Bc
last

Ren
1

12.

12.

06.9

04.

04.

1 st

LETTS HOME DECORATOR

WALLS
& WOODWORK

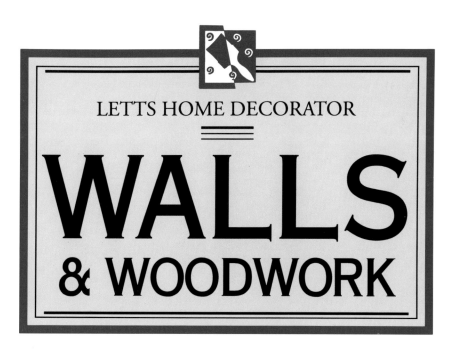

LETTS HOME DECORATOR

WALLS & WOODWORK

MIKE LAWRENCE
AND
FRED MILSON

CHARLES LETTS
Letts
of London®
FOUNDED 1796

First published in 1993
by Charles Letts & Co Ltd
Letts of London House, Parkgate Road
London SW11 4NQ

Designed and edited by
Anness Publishing Limited
Boundary Row Studios
1 Boundary Row
London SE1 8HP

ISBN 1 85238 379 8

A CIP catalogue record for this book is
available from the British Library.

'Letts' is a registered trademark of
Charles Letts & Co Ltd

Editorial Director: Joanna Lorenz
Project Editor: Judith Simons
Text Editor: Charles Moxham
Design: Millions Design
Photographer: John Freeman
Illustration: King & King Associates

Printed and bound in Spain

PUBLISHER'S NOTE

The authors and publishers have made every effort to ensure
that all instructions contained within this book are accurate
and safe, and cannot accept liability for any resulting injury,
damage or loss to persons or property however it may arise. If
in any doubt as to the correct procedure to follow for any home
improvements task, seek professional advice.

CONTENTS

INTRODUCTION

 Walls, ceilings and woodwork constitute the lion's share of your home decorating workload, so this book is dedicated to explaining everything you need to know about decorating them.

It introduces you to the various materials you can use, and then deals with every home decorator's least favourite chore – removing all the existing decorations and preparing the surfaces underneath them ready to receive their new finish.

With the preparation over, you can move on to planning your new colour schemes, and in the next chapter you will find a wealth of practical advice to help you make the right decisions for every room in the house, and to select the best materials to meet a range of performance criteria.

The book goes on to describe in detail the tools, materials and techniques to use for painting, varnishing, staining and creating special paint effects. The final chapter covers all the ins and outs of paperhanging, from basic techniques to dealing with awkward areas such as window reveals, chimney breasts, ceilings and stairwells.

Throughout the book you will find precise step-by-step picture sequences that show you in detail how each individual job should be tackled, and there are also clear diagrams and charts to help you with everything from setting up access equipment safely to estimating materials. You will find each chapter packed with expert advice, handy tips and product information – in fact, everything you need to know to get your walls, ceilings and woodwork into perfect shape and looking better than you ever dreamed possible.

Successful decorating is the sum of many elements: careful preparation work, mastering a few basic techniques and matching the right materials to the decorating task in hand.

BASIC TOOLS AND EQUIPMENT

Apart from specialist painting and paperhanging equipment, you will need a range of general-purpose drilling, cutting, filling and fixing tools to enable you to carry out many of the jobs featured in this book. Some you may already have in your tool kit; others will be well worth buying for present and future use. In particular, invest in some simple safety equipment: stout gloves to protect your hands, and safety goggles to guard your eyes from dust, splashes and flying debris.

1 Portable work bench
2 Claw hammer
3 Bolster (wide) chisel
4 Club hammer
5 Spirit level
6 Safety spectacles
7 Gloves
8 Electric chop saw
9 Cordless electric drill/screwdriver
10 Battery charger for cordless drill
11 Drill bits, screwdriver attachments and chuck key for cordless drill
12 Angle grinder
13 Discs and abrasive pads for angle grinder
14 Coping saw
15 Tenon saw (backsaw)
16 Slotted and cross-head screwdrivers
17 Filling knives
18 Cutting knife
19 Retractable steel tape measure
20 Steel rule
21 Pencil
22 Try square
23 Nails
24 Pins
25 Screws
26 Wallplugs

PREPARATION

Anyone who has ever renovated an old house will have come across the cumulative school of decorating: walls boasting three, four or more layers of wallpaper, each pasted directly on top of its predecessor, or else featuring successive layers of distemper, often in horribly conflicting colours. With little or no time spent on preparation work prior to redecoration, the result was seldom a total success and frequently a visual disaster.

Nowadays no one expects to strip existing emulsion (latex) paint before applying a fresh coat, but then modern paints are far more stable than their predecessors. However, few modern wallcoverings will tolerate being papered over and many other modern decorative finishes will perform well only if they are applied to a sound surface. So taking stock of the present condition of your walls, ceilings and woodwork is a vital first step towards making their future finish a success.

Each surface, be it wood, plaster, metal and, as here, bare masonry, will need to be prepared in a particular way to ensure that the new finish looks great and lasts.

ASSESSING THE SITUATION

When you decide to redecorate a room, knowing what you want to achieve is only half the battle. Between the dream and the reality lies a great divide: getting there.

This not only involves taking the obvious steps such as deciding what new colour scheme to select and what decorative products to choose. More importantly, it means evaluating what you will be up against in practical terms, since successful decorating is like the proverbial iceberg: nine-tenths of the business lies concealed beneath the surface.

RENOVATE OR REDECORATE?

If the state of a room's decorations is basically sound, you may need to do little more than give the walls, ceiling and woodwork a thorough wash to freshen them up – assuming that they are decorated with washable materials. The main exceptions are printed wallpapers, which may be able to tolerate a light sponging, and certain fabric wallcoverings which can often benefit from a light brushing or vacuum cleaning.

If you feel that the room merits more drastic action, painted surfaces generally need just a new coat of paint, but wallcoverings will have to be removed unless they are specifically designed or suitable for overpainting. Other surface materials such as timber cladding (siding) and tiles pose their own individual problems. Furthermore, each surface in the room needs looking at closely to ensure that it is in good condition before redecoration can begin.

The answer is to look at the ceiling, walls and woodwork in turn.

ASSESSING THE CEILING CONDITION

If the ceiling is of lath-and-plaster construction, press upwards against its surface to see whether it is showing any sign of bowing; this would indicate that the plaster key above the laths has failed. You may be able to rescue small areas, if you can easily gain access to the upper surface of the ceiling, by propping up the bulge from underneath and then pouring quick-setting plaster over the laths to form a new key. However, if the bowing is more severe it is generally better to have the ceiling completely replaced with a new plasterboard (dry wall or gypsum board) surface.

CEILING TYPES

Most homes have plastered ceilings. In homes built more than about sixty years ago the ceiling surface was formed by nailing closely spaced slim timber strips called laths across the ceiling joists and then pressing a coat of plaster against their undersides. The plaster was forced up between the laths to form a key on their upper surfaces which held the ceiling up.

During the 1920s, what we know as plasterboard (dry wall or gypsum board) was developed for use as ceiling and wall surfaces. This consists of a hard gypsum-plaster core sandwiched between two sheets of stout absorbent paper to form a rigid board that is fixed directly to ceiling joists and wall frames. Once in place, the plaster-board is then given a skim coat of plaster to hide the joints and provide a smooth flat surface for subsequent decoration. It is obviously quicker to install than a lath-and-plaster surface, and also dries out much more quickly than conventional wet plasterwork.

Tongued-and-grooved timber ceilings, once a popular alternative to lath-and-plaster, can be seen in older, usually nineteenth-century, homes. If found in more modern homes, the boards are likely to be a decorative addition concealing an old plastered ceiling surface, rather than forming the actual ceiling itself.

IDENTIFYING DISTEMPER

In older homes, be on the lookout for distemper on walls and ceiling surfaces. Its powdery surface cannot be painted or papered over directly unless it is either sealed or completely removed by scrubbing.

The commonest fault with plasterboard (dry-wall or gypsum-board) ceilings is cracking, often along the wall–ceiling junction and sometimes also along the joints between adjacent boards if these were not properly taped when the ceiling was first put up. Do not fill these cracks with hard filler; they will simply open up again as the ceiling structure flexes. Instead, use a flexible decorators' mastic (caulking) to fill the surface cracks, and consider putting up coving to conceal the perimeter ones.

If the ceiling has been papered, expect to have to remove this unless it has a painted finish which can simply be overpainted. In the latter case, look for bubbles or lifting seams, and stick down any that you find with wallpaper paste.

If the ceiling has a flat paint finish, look for any sign of flaking or dusting. Flaky patches will need scraping or sanding down. Dusting, however, suggests that the ceiling has been decorated with distemper, which is usually only found in old houses. The washable type can be sealed with a coat of stabilizing solution, but non-washable distemper must be scrubbed off with water before the ceiling can be redecorated.

If the ceiling has been given a textured finish, you have two choices: to repaint it if you like the effect, or else to replace it. You can remove powder-type finishes using a steam wallpaper stripper (a long, hot and messy job), while textured emulsion (latex) paints can be stripped off using specially formulated chemicals. However, a quicker solution is to have a skim coat of plaster applied over the textured finish to create a new smooth ceiling surface.

If the ceiling is boarded or has been covered with polystyrene tiles, you must decide whether you want to keep the surface or replace it with something else. Taking down a boarded ceiling is usually quite straightforward, but tiles can be very difficult to remove without damaging the underlying surface. It is often quicker to put up a complete new plasterboard ceiling surface to conceal them; you will probably need professional help to do this.

ASSESSING THE WALL CONDITION

With solid walls, check that the plaster is sound by tapping the surface with your knuckles. Any areas that sound hollow will have to be replastered before the wall is redecorated. Smaller blemishes such as dents and cracks will need patching with filler.

With plasterboard (dry-wall or gypsum-board) walls, cracks may open up as they do with ceilings if the joints between adjacent boards were not taped. Fill these cracks with decorators' mastic (caulking) rather than a hard-setting filler. Patch small holes in the board with scrim tape and filler, or cut the board back to the adjacent studs and nail in a new patch if it is badly damaged.

As far as the wall's existing decorative finish is concerned, your options are broadly similar to those for ceilings. You can generally apply any new finish over a painted wall, but wallcoverings will have to be stripped off unless they are designed or suitable for overpainting.

TYPES OF WOODWORK

The woodwork in a typical room will fall into three groups: window frames, doors, and decorative trims such as skirting boards (baseboards), architraves, dadoes (chair rails) and picture rails. They will need little more than a fresh coat of paint, varnish or stain unless the existing finish is in very poor condition or successive layers have built up to such an extent that they are causing doors and windows to bind or are obscuring the detail of decorative mouldings. If this is the case, or you want to change the existing finish for something completely different, you will have to remove the old finish before you can redecorate.

Your woodwork may of course be in need of rather more than just a fresh coat of paint. Physical damage may have resulted in dents and chips to the surface of the wood itself, and cracks may have opened up between joints. Both will need filling before the new finish is applied.

WALL TYPES

Walls are either solid masonry or built with plasterboard (dry wall or gypsum board) on a timber framework. Solid walls will be plastered to a thickness of between 10 to 20mm ($\frac{3}{8}$ to $\frac{3}{4}$in), while plasterboard will generally have a thin skim of finish plaster.

In some older properties you may find timber-framed walls finished with the same lath-and-plaster construction used for ceilings before the introduction of plasterboard. Such walls tend to suffer from the same defects as lath-and-plaster ceilings, especially the loss of the plaster key.

TESTING PLASTER

Where old plaster looks suspect, test it by tapping it. A hollow sound indicates that the bond to the wall or ceiling has failed and some patching will be required.

PREPARATION EQUIPMENT

You will need various tools for preparation work depending on the type of surface you are working on and the type of finish you are dealing with. A hot-air gun is a useful tool for removing paint; use with scrapers on flat surfaces or special shavehooks if removing paint or varnish from intricate mouldings, such as architraves or dado (chair) rails. Scrapers are also used to strip ordinary wallpaper, but with washable and painted paper you will need a scoring tool to perforate the surface and allow the water to penetrate and soften the old paste. A steam stripper will speed up the process considerably. Abrasive papers are multi-purpose; always keep a stock handy in various grades. Filling knives, a plasterer's float and scrim tape will be needed for minor and major repairs to plaster surfaces.

1 **Hot-air gun**
2 **Mitre block**
3 **Shavehooks**
4 **Scrapers**
5 **Abrasive papers**
6 **Filling knife**
7 **Plasterer's float**
8 **Scrim tape**
9 **Scoring tools**
10 **Steam stripper**

PREPARING WALLS & CEILINGS

Whatever surface you are redecorating, the purpose of preparation is to remove any loose or unstable material from that surface — including old decorative finishes where appropriate — and to leave it clean, dry, smooth and free from any faults that could spoil the new finish. Skimping on preparation is the commonest cause of disappointing results when decorating; unfortunately, it is by far the most time-consuming and least rewarding part of the job, which is why it is so often either done badly or not at all. Here is what you *should* be doing by way of proper surface preparation.

PAINTED PLASTER

Whatever new finish you intend to apply, your first step must always be to wash the surface down thoroughly. It is surprising how much airborne dirt and grease collects on even a smooth, flat wall or ceiling surface. In addition, there will be localized areas which suffer from splashes, hand- or fingerprints and other random marks.

Use either proprietary sugar soap – the best product for the job – or a hot solution of strong household detergent for washing down wall and ceiling surfaces. Wear rubber gloves to protect your hands, and if washing a ceiling always wear safety spectacles or goggles to guard against splashes in the eyes. Add a cap or similar headgear if you wish to protect your hair. Put down dust sheets to keep drips off floorcoverings, move the furniture into the centre of the room and cover it with plastic sheeting.

Wash the surfaces with a cloth or sponge, starting at the bottom of walls or at one edge of a ceiling. Work in areas of about a square metre (yard) at a time, rinsing off the washed

area with clean water before moving on to the next one. When you have completed the job, give the whole surface another wash down with more clean water, working from the top downwards on walls, and then leave it to dry.

If the paint shows signs of flaking off at any point, scrape or sand away the loose material and touch-in bare patches with a little emulsion (latex) paint to avoid leaving a depression which will show up when the surface is repainted. If the paint has a crusty appearance, this may be the result of a fault known as efflorescence. It occurs when moisture in the wall brings dissolved mineral salts to the surface and evaporates, leaving the salts as a dry deposit under the paint films. Scrape it off ready for repainting, and keep an eye on the wall in case the problem recurs; it could be a sign of rising or penetrating damp.

Lastly, attend to any dents and cracks in the wall surface. Use the tip of a filling knife to rake out loose material and to undercut the edges slightly so the filler will adhere more effectively. Brush out any remaining dust and dampen the area (a small garden spray gun is ideal for this) before filling the defect with plaster or proprietary filler. Use the same technique to fill cracks between boards on timber-framed partition walls and on plasterboard (dry-wall or gypsum-board) ceilings, and also to fill gaps between walls and wooden frames or trims. Bridge cracks along the join between walls and ceilings with scrim tape bedded in a little filler and skimmed over with more filler for an invisible repair. Do not worry about hairline cracks, which paint will fill and wallpaper will bridge. (See *Repairing Damage*, pages 25–31, for more details.)

If you plan to repaint the surface, that is all you need to do. However, if you intend to hang a wallcovering there are two more steps to undertake. The first is to roughen the surface slightly, especially if it has an eggshell or gloss finish, using fine wet-and-dry abrasive paper. The second is to size it with diluted wallpaper paste to improve the slip and adhesion of the new wallcovering. Let this dry before you start paperhanging.

SEALING OLD PLASTER

To seal highly porous plaster, brush on a coat of diluted PVA building adhesive or a proprietary plaster sealer. Use stabilizing solution to seal old distempered surfaces.

USING REINFORCING TAPE

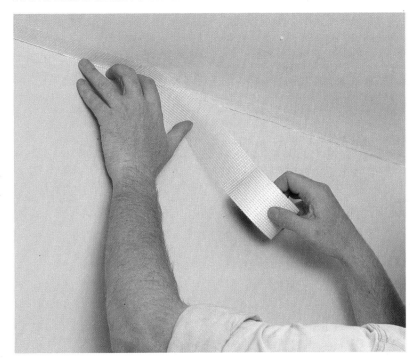

1 Use self-adhesive scrim tape to reinforce troublesome cracks such as those between walls and ceilings. First press the tape into place.

2 Then apply filler over the tape along the wall and ceiling edges to fill in the mesh structure of the reinforcing tape.

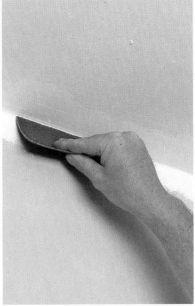

3 When the filler has hardened, use abrasive paper to smooth the surface of the filled area and to remove any nibs or ridges.

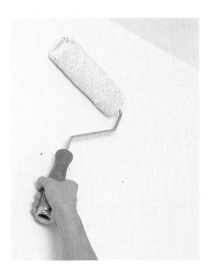

4 Finally paint over the area to conceal the filler and leave a repair which will not crack if movement between floor and ceiling recurs.

PATTERNED WALLPAPER

Walls and ceilings may be covered with patterned or painted paper. The former will have to be removed whatever new finish you intend to use, although you might get away with painting over ordinary printed wallpaper (but not washables or vinyls – see page 17) if you want an instant budget facelift, so long as the paper is firmly stuck down and has no lifting edges or seams. If you are tempted to try this, test the paint first on an inconspicuous area of wall to see whether the printing inks are fast; always seal any metallic inks first with a spirit-based sealer.

How you strip patterned wallpaper depends on what type of product it is. Ordinary printed papers will absorb water readily, so soaking them with a garden spray gun or sponge will quickly soften the paste and allow the paper to be scraped off easily with a broad-bladed scraper. Once you have removed all the paper, wash the wall surface down with clean water to remove any remaining nibs of paper and the residue of the old paste.

Removing old wallpaper will reveal a plain surface, which may or may not have been painted. Examine it carefully for defects,

especially if you plan to paint rather than paper it. Fill cracks and hollows with filler as described for *Painted Plaster* (see page 14), overfilling the defects slightly and then sanding the filler down flush with its surroundings when dry. (See *Repairing Damage*, pages 25–31, for details of how to tackle more serious defects.)

If the surface is bare plaster that feels powdery to the touch, seal it with a coat of stabilizing primer or diluted PVA adhesive/sealer. If it has a paint finish that you can rub off with a damp cloth, this may be distemper (see page 15).

STRIPPING WALLPAPER

1 With ordinary printed and washable papers, start by scoring the surface with a proprietary tool to help water to penetrate and soften the old paste.

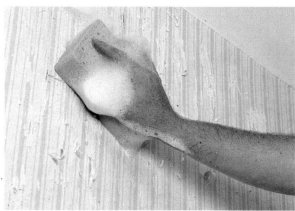

2 Wet the wall with a sponge or a garden spray gun. Adding a little household detergent to the water makes it soak into the paper more quickly.

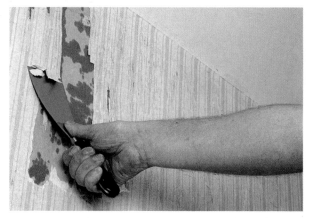

3 Use a broad-bladed scraper, which is stiffer than a filling knife, to scrape the old paper off the wall. Wet the paper repeatedly, if necessary.

USING A STEAM STRIPPER

1 Speed up the soaking process by using a steam stripper to force steam into the old paste. Start by running a perforating wheel over the surface.

2 Then press the steam plate against the paper for a while, lift it aside and scrape off the paper. Steam the next area as you scrape the first.

STRIPPING WASHABLES AND VINYLS

Washable wallpapers have a clear plastic protective coating over the printed paper surface, so water will penetrate only if this film is scored or perforated first, and then not easily. They are best removed with the aid of a special wheeled perforating tool and a steam wallpaper stripper. This forces steam rather than water through the perforations to soften the paste, and works much more efficiently than simply soaking it.

Vinyls have the pattern printed on and fused into the plastic layer, which is bonded to a plain paper backing for ease of hanging – and stripping. You simply peel off the printed plastic layer dry, then soak and scrape off the paper backing like a printed paper. Do not be tempted to leave this backing on the wall as a lining for subsequent paperhanging; the paste on the new paper will soften the old backing paper and cause unsightly blisters which will be impossible to remove or disguise.

PAINTED WALLPAPER

With painted papers you have two decorating options; to apply more paint, or to strip the paper and apply an alternative decorative finish. To prepare for repainting, wash down the surface as for painted plaster, and stick down any raised seams or edges you find with a little wallpaper paste. If there are any dry bubbles visible, slit them open with a sharp knife and brush some stiff wallpaper paste into the slits, then press flat and leave to dry. If, however, you decide to remove the paper, treat it as you would a washable wallpaper, perforating the surface paint film first and then using a steam stripper to soften the paste so the paper can be stripped off.

OTHER WALLCOVERINGS

You may be faced with stripping other types of wallcovering in the course of redecorating a room – flocks, fabrics or a unique all-plastic wallcovering made of foamed polyethylene, for example.

Flock wallpapers may be of two types: traditional printed wallpaper or a vinyl. Strip the former as for ordinary printed papers, and peel off the plastic surface of the latter as for other vinyl wallcoverings.

Fabric wallcoverings can be more difficult to remove, since many are hung with heavy-duty ready-mixed pastes. First, try peeling off the fabric layer dry. If this does not work, use a steam wallpaper stripper to soften the paste and allow the wallcovering to be removed more easily.

Foamed polyethylene, a lightweight wallcovering, does not have a paper backing. It is hung by pasting the wall, not the wallcovering, and can simply be peeled off again when you want to replace it.

REMOVING TEXTURED EMULSION (LATEX) PAINT

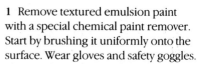

1 Remove textured emulsion paint with a special chemical paint remover. Start by brushing it uniformly onto the surface. Wear gloves and safety goggles.

2 Leave the remover to penetrate the coating for the recommended time, then use a stripping knife to scrape it off. Deposit scrapings in a tin.

TEXTURED FINISHES

Three-dimensional textured effects are a popular decorative choice for ceilings and, less commonly, for walls. The original type comes either in the form of a powder which is mixed with water to a rich creamy consistency, or else ready-mixed in a tub. It is brushed liberally onto the surface being decorated, and is then worked on before it sets with a variety of tools to create regular or random surface patterns. Once it hardens, it can be painted with emulsion (latex) or solvent-based (alkyd) paint.

A more recent introduction is texture paint, which is a thicker-than-usual emulsion paint applied and textured in a similar way to the powder/ready-mix finishes mentioned earlier. It is available in white and some pastel shades, and can be overpainted if desired. The main difference is that it is applied more thinly and so will not take the more dramatic three-dimensional effects that can be created with the original texturing products.

If you want to keep an existing textured finish, you can simply wash the surface down in the usual way and apply a fresh coat of paint. Use a coarse roller for low-relief textures and a brush for deeper reliefs, working the paint well into the nooks and crannies. However, if you want a change of material, you have two options: to remove the textured finish or to cover it up. Which you choose will depend on what type of textured finish it is.

With the original thicker products, it is worth trying to scrape the finish off, especially if it was originally applied to a painted surface. Test a small area first to see if it will come away easily. If it does, carry on scraping, but bear in mind the possibility that some older textured finishes contain asbestos fibre, so the dust could be hazardous to your health. Wear a dust mask at all times, and bag up all the debris carefully when you have finished. For this reason, you should *never* attempt to sand off an old textured finish.

If scraping proves ineffective, use a steam wallpaper stripper – by far the quickest way of removing this type of finish, especially if it has been painted over. Work on a small area at a time, depositing the softened scrapings in a bucket or box as you remove them. Then wash the surface down thoroughly with clean water before redecorating.

If a steam stripper does not work, this indicates that the finish is probably a modern texture paint, which will have to be stripped using a specially formulated chemical paint stripper. Work this well into the surface with a brush and leave it to work for the recommended time before scraping off the softened texture. If you are working on a ceiling, be sure to wear at least a pair of safety goggles, and ideally a face mask and cap too, to guard against splashes.

All these methods are messy and time-consuming, and there is no guarantee that you will be left with a smooth, blemish-free surface at the end. A quicker if more expensive solution is to have a skim coat of fresh plaster applied over the whole surface to conceal the texture, or to put up a new plasterboard (dry-wall or gypsum-board) ceiling if you can easily locate the original joist positions.

TILES

Tiles of various types are frequently used on walls and, to a lesser extent, on ceilings. Ceramic wall tiles are the most common, and are often used on small areas such as splashbacks as well as to cover whole walls. Cork tiles are also popular for walls, while polystyrene tiles are widely used on ceilings. How you tackle them depends on whether you want to retain or replace them.

Ceramic tiles are virtually indestructible, although it is possible for the odd tile to become dislodged if not properly bedded in its adhesive, and impacts can crack individual tiles. If either of these problems has occurred and you want to keep the tiled area, it is relatively simple to put things right. To replace a loose tile, chip away as much of the old adhesive and grout as possible with a cold chisel and hammer, then spread some fresh ready-mixed tile adhesive (available in tubes for repair work) on the back of the tile and press it into place. Regrout round its perimeter when the adhesive has set.

To remove a damaged tile, again use a small cold chisel and hammer, working from the centre of the tile outwards to chip away the broken pieces and the old adhesive. Fit a new tile as described earlier.

One problem with ceramic-tiled walls is that the grout lines often become discoloured with time. The best remedy for this is to rake out the grout with an old screwdriver or similar tool, and then apply fresh grout. Alternatively, you can paint the grout with special grout paint, or try bleaching out the discoloration with household bleach. Neither is as effective as regrouting.

If you decide to replace the tiles with something else, think carefully before starting work. For a start it will be very hard work and you will probably be left with a wall missing large chunks of plaster in some places and adorned with lumps of rock-hard adhesive in others. The use of a steam wallpaper stripper may help to soften the old adhesive once you have chipped off the tiles, but there are sure to be some extensive repairs to carry out before the wall is fit for redecoration. Tiles on plasterboard (dry wall or gypsum board) are almost impossible to remove without wrecking the board, and it is often quicker to pull off the entire board with the tiles and then put up fresh boarding.

The alternatives to removing tiles are cover-ups. You can tile on top of existing tiles if you simply want a change of look rather

REPLACING A CRACKED TILE

1 Chip off the cracked tile with a small cold chisel, working towards the centre. Drill holes in the tile first, if necessary, to create a starting point.

2 Remove as much of the old tile adhesive as possible with a stripping knife or cold chisel. Do not worry if you make a few holes in the plaster.

3 Spread tile adhesive thinly on the wall and on the tile back, and press the tile into place. Check that it is level with its neighbours, using spacers if necessary, then grout.

than a change of finish; modern tile adhesives are strong enough to stick even to existing tiles. You can fix decorative wallboards to the surface with panel adhesive. Lastly, you can fix plasterboard to battens (furring strips) fixed to the tiled wall to create a brand new wall surface.

Cork tiles pose a different set of problems. If you simply want to refresh their looks, scrub them down and leave to dry before sealing with clear or coloured varnish. If you prefer to do away with them altogether, do *not* try to remove them. They will have been stuck up with contact adhesive which is virtually impossible to remove, and you will be left with a wall covered with random lumps of cork and unsightly bands of rubbery adhesive. Instead, leave them intact and hang heavy-duty lining paper over them. This can then be simply painted or used as a base for a new wallcovering.

Polystyrene tiles can also be difficult to replace. They used to be stuck up with five blobs of adhesive until fire officers discovered that in the event of a fire, dollops of burning molten polystyrene would fall from the ceiling and simply spread the fire. Now all polystyrene tiles are treated to increase their fire resistance, and are stuck up with a continuous bed of adhesive, making them all the more difficult to remove. Unless you find that the tiles are stuck with blobs and are prepared to chip them away one by one, it is far quicker to adopt the cover-up approach again and put up a new plasterboard ceiling to conceal them. If, however, you decide to retain the tiles and want to paint them, *never* use a solvent-based paint, which will dramatically increase the risk of flames spreading in the event of a fire. Use ordinary emulsion (latex) paint, or better still, a special fire-retardant paint.

CLADDING (SIDING)

The last decorative surface you are likely to encounter is cladding – either natural timber or manufactured wallboards. The former comes in a range of profiles, and is generally pinned to a framework of battens (furring strips) attached to the wall surface. The board surface may be painted, varnished or stained, and if the cladding is to be retained and redecorated this should be treated as for other woodwork in the room (see *Preparing Woodwork*, pages 21–23, for more details). If it is to be removed, start by prising off any trim beading round the clad area, then simply lever the boards away from the battens with a crowbar or similar tool. If the battens are fixed with screws driven into wallplugs, unscrew them carefully, then fill the plug holes with filler. If they were put up with masonry nails, try levering the nails out, but be prepared for some extensive localized damage to the wall which will have to be patched up before redecorating. If they will not budge, break away the battens and hammer the nails right into the wall. Fill the depression and sand down the surface with abrasive paper to prevent the nail head showing through the newly decorated surface.

Wallboards are sheets of hardboard or plywood with a veneered or plastic-coated face that is often made to resemble timber cladding or ceramic tiles. They may also be fixed to battens, in which case you can prise everything off as already described if you are replacing them. If, however, the boards have been stuck directly to the wall surface with panel adhesive (this can be detected by tapping the boards – they will sound solid rather than hollow, as they do on battens), you will not be able to shift them. Instead, decorate over them. You can either paint the boards (which will not disguise any decorative grooving) or cover them with heavy-duty lining paper to provide a surface for painting or paperhanging.

Timber cladding (siding) is usually pinned to a framework of battens (furring strips) nailed to the wall surface. It provides a hardwearing wall surface, especially between a dado (chair) rail and the skirting board (baseboard), the area of the wall most susceptible to damage. Cladding can be removed, but an easier alternative is to refresh the finish with a new coat of paint or stain/varnish.

PREPARING WOODWORK

Preparing woodwork for redecoration is a lot less complicated than tackling walls and ceilings, since there are fewer decorative options to deal with. However, it can still be a time-consuming process, especially if existing finishes have to be removed, and as with walls and ceilings poor preparation means poor results. This is particularly important with a room's woodwork, since the eye is naturally drawn to features such as doors, windows, picture and dado rails (chair rails), architraves and skirting boards (baseboards), and any visible surface blemishes are therefore that much harder to disguise.

Modern paints, varnishes and stains are without a doubt much easier to use and also perform better than their forerunners, and because of this there is the temptation to expect them to perform miracles in any situation. However, to give of their best they must be applied carefully to well-prepared surfaces. So the first priority is to take a close look at what is there already and assess its condition.

PAINTED WOODWORK

Before starting any actual preparation work, inspect the paint surface carefully. If it is in good physical condition, with no visible chips or dents, and there is no evidence of an excessive build-up of paint on the surface, then you can simply wash down and key the surface ready to receive a fresh coat of paint. Use sugar soap or strong household detergent, which will remove dirt and grease, finger marks and the like, and rinse down with clean water. Use improvised tools such as an old toothbrush to reach into corners and to clean out the recesses of timber mouldings. If the finish has a high gloss, flatten this by sanding the surface lightly with fine wet-and-dry abrasive paper, used wet, and then wipe the surface down again with clean water. This will ensure the best possible adhesion of the new paint to the existing finish.

If the painted surface has suffered localized damage but is otherwise sound, wash it down then tackle the blemishes. If bare wood is exposed, carefully cut away any damaged wood fibres with a sharp knife and sand the wood smooth, feathering the edges of the paint finish surrounding the blemish to avoid any sharp edges that will show through the new finish. Use a little wood filler if necessary to repair the damaged area, then touch in the blemish with wood primer, then undercoat, to replace the missing paint layers. Finally use the chosen topcoat to bring the level of the paint over the blemish up flush with the surrounding paintwork ready for a final overall coat of new paint.

The existing finish may be in poor condition, with worn patches, flaking and extensive surface damage. Previous coats of paint may also have built up to such an extent that moving parts – doors and windows – are binding in their frames and the detail on decorative mouldings has become obscured. In these situations, it is time to strip off the existing finish and build up a new paint system from scratch. Choose this route, too, if you want a change of finish – for example, stain or varnish instead of paint. How the job is tackled depends on the new finish you want to apply and on the type of surface you are working on. (See *Stripping Old Finishes*, pages 22–23, for more details.)

REPAIRING ROTTEN WOOD

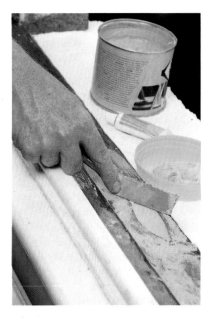

1 If you find rotten wood in window or door frames, dig out all the loose material with a sharp knife, cutting back to solid wood.

2 Brush out loose debris, then apply a coat of special resin-based wood hardener to stabilize and protect the surrounding wood.

3 Repair the damage using quick-setting wood filler, a two-part product which is mixed up immediately prior to use and which sets rock hard.

VARNISHED WOODWORK

Woodwork that has been given a clear finish is probably the easiest to prepare for redecoration. It can be given a fresh coat of varnish to restore its surface appearance, or can be painted over for a change of finish. As with paintwork, wash the surface down thoroughly first, then inspect the surface for localized blemishes. Touch in chips and scratches with fresh varnish (and wood filler if necessary), key the surface with fine wet-and-dry abrasive paper and rinse.

Varnish finishes can also build up in thickness to the point where doors and windows bind in their frames. If this is the case the solution is the same as for paint: remove the old finish ready for a new one to be applied. (Again, see *Stripping Old Finishes*, this and next page.)

If revarnishing the wood, you can use either a satin or high-gloss finish, irrespective of the type used previously. Remember that a high-gloss finish will accentuate any defects in the wood surface; choose a satin finish instead if yours is less than perfect.

If painting the surface, treat the existing varnish as a primer and simply apply undercoat and topcoat (or a one-coat paint) directly over it.

STAINED WOODWORK

You may have woodwork that has been given a pigmented finish to change the colour of the wood or to enhance its grain. This may have been achieved with a coloured varnish, or by the use of wood stains followed by clear varnish. You can test which you have by stripping the finish from a small test area using varnish remover; this will remove both clear and coloured varnish, so if the wood colour remains unchanged you will know that a wood stain has been used.

Prepare the surface as described for varnished wood, washing down and keying it ready for redecoration. If you intend using the same finish, touch-in blemishes in old coloured varnish with the new finish, and use diluted wood stain to disguise chips and scratches in stained wood before applying clear varnish over the top. The reason for using diluted stain is that you have better control of the colouring process, using several coats to bring the colour to a perfect match with the surrounding woodwork. If you use undiluted stain there is a risk that the blemish will end up looking much darker than the rest of the woodwork.

As with clear varnished woodwork, you can paint over both coloured varnish and varnished stain if you want a complete change of finish. If, however, you want to keep the look of the wood but you want to change its colour, you will have to remove the existing finish and, in the case of wood stains, bleach the existing stain for a lighter-coloured finish; for a darker one, you simply apply more stain to the stripped wood before revarnishing it. (See *Stripping Old Finishes*, below, for more details.)

STRIPPING OLD FINISHES

You have two basic choices when it comes to stripping old finishes from wood – heat and chemicals – and which you select will depend on two main factors.

The first is the type of finish you intend to apply once you have removed the old one. Heat stripping, whether using an old-fashioned blowlamp (blowtorch) or an electric hot-air gun, almost always results in some charring of the wood surface, and this would obviously mar the look of a clear or coloured varnish finish. For this reason, heat stripping is best used when you intend to paint the wood. Otherwise, opt for chemical strippers. You will also have to use chemicals to strip paint close to glass in windows and doors, since the heat from a blowlamp or hot-air gun may crack it.

The second factor to consider is cost. Heat stripping is obviously a relatively inexpensive technique. Chemical strippers, by contrast, are expensive if used over large areas, and if you want to expose a lot of bare woodwork it may be worth having movable items such as doors stripped professionally. Also, consider replacing fittings like skirting boards (baseboards) and architraves with new wood rather than going through the trouble of stripping them. Weigh up the cost options before deciding which course to take.

PRISING OFF ARCHITRAVES
If mouldings such as architraves are badly clogged with paint, it is often quicker to prise them off and replace them with new wood.

HEAT STRIPPING

This works by softening the paint or varnish film so it can be scraped off the wood. On flat surfaces, play the blowlamp flame or gun airstream over the surface for a few seconds until it starts to bubble up, then withdraw the heat and scrape off the blistered finish with a flat-bladed scraper. Deposit the scrapings in a tin for safety, rather than letting them drop to the floor; they are hot and could ignite dust sheets or damage floorcoverings. Apply more heat if necessary to thick films, moving on to the next area when you get down to the bare wood.

On mouldings and other areas with intricate surface detail, use a shavehook to scrape the paint from the recesses, plus improvised tools such as a slim screwdriver to reach parts the shavehook cannot penetrate. On surfaces such as panelled doors, tackle the mouldings first so that the paint on the surrounding flat areas provides some protection to the wood and helps prevent excessive charring.

When you have removed all the old finish, sand the bare wood down thoroughly with abrasive paper to remove any nibs of old paint and to leave the surface flat and smooth ready for the new finish.

Whether you are using a blowlamp or a hot-air gun, take great care not to burn yourself or set fire to anything as you work. Wear leather gloves to protect your hands, and set the lamp or gun down well away from any flammable materials, allowing it to cool down thoroughly before putting it away at the end of the job.

CHEMICAL STRIPPERS

Chemical paint and varnish removers contain agents that dissolve the old finish when they are brushed on, again allowing it to be lifted with a scraper or shavehook. They are the obvious choice when you want to give the stripped wood a new clear or pigmented finish instead of paint, although two or more applications may be needed to lift thick accumulations from heavily moulded or detailed surfaces. There are two types: liquid strippers generally contain methylene dichloride, while paste types are usually based on sodium hydroxide – the type used by commercial firms to strip doors, painted furniture and the like. Both types must be used with care to avoid splashes, and good ventilation is essential when using methylene dichloride types. Whichever type you are using, follow the maker's instructions

carefully at all times, especially with regard to neutralizing the stripper after the old finish has been removed. If any traces of the chemical stripper remain, they will attack and spoil the new finish, so thorough rinsing with either water or white (mineral) spirit is essential before the wood is sanded down ready for its new finish.

When you have removed the old finish, you may find that the surface of the wood has a very grainy feel to it. If you are repainting, it is a good idea to use a grain filler to create a smooth flat surface ready for the new paint system to be applied. Mix this up and use a spatula to draw the filler across the wood at right angles to the grain direction, then sand it smooth when it has hardened.

BLEACHING STAINED WOOD

If the stripped wood has been previously stained and you want to alter its colour to a lighter shade, use special wood bleach (not ordinary household bleach) to lift the stain. Follow the manufacturer's instructions carefully to avoid patchy results, and ensure that the bleach is completely rinsed off before applying the new stain.

STRIPPING MOULDINGS

Use a hot-air gun and a shavehook to strip paint from intricate mouldings. The shaped head of the shavehook will reach into even narrow grooves.

REPAIRING LOCALIZED DAMAGE

Once you have stripped the old paint from the surface of a moulding, sand it down smooth and make good any surface defects with wood filler.

PREPARATION CHECKLIST

EXISTING SURFACE	CONDITION	TREATMENT
PLASTER	Dry, sound	Prime with diluted emulsion (latex) paint
	Dusty/distempered	Wash off and apply stabilizing primer
	Painted	Wash down and repaint *or* abrade surface and apply size if hanging wallpaper
PLASTERBOARD (DRY WALL OR GYPSUM BOARD)	New	Diluted emulsion (latex) paint or drywall sealer (US)
	Painted	Wash down, repaint *or* abrade surface and apply size if hanging wallpaper
WALLCOVERINGS	Printed wallpaper	Strip off and wash down
	Painted paper	Repaint if sound *or* strip off and wash down
	Washable paper	Strip off and wash down
	Vinyl wallcovering	Strip off top layer dry, remove backing paper and wash down
	Fabric wallcovering	Strip off dry and wash down
	Foamed polyethylene	Peel off dry and wash down
TEXTURED FINISHES	–	Wash down and repaint *or* strip off
WOOD	Bare	Apply wood primer or primer/undercoat
	Painted	Wash down, abrade and repaint *or* strip and redecorate
	Varnished	Wash down, abrade and revarnish *or* cover with new paint *or* strip off, stain and revarnish
	Stained and varnished	Wash down, abrade and revarnish *or* cover with new paint *or* strip off, bleach or darken, then revarnish
IRON AND STEEL	Rusty	Remove rust and apply primer (see page 30)
	New	Apply zinc chromate primer
	Galvanized	Apply calcium plumbate primer
ALUMINIUM	–	Apply zinc chromate/phosphate primer
COPPER/BRASS	Discoloured	Clean with metal polish
	New	No primer necessary
PLASTIC	–	Wash down, abrade and apply multi-purpose primer
TILES	Ceramic	Replace lose or broken tiles and regrout, if necessary, *or* lay new tiles over old ones *or* fix plasterboard over tiled surface and redecorate
	Cork	Wash down and seal with varnish *or* hang lining paper over tiles and redecorate
	Polystyrene	Paint with emulsion (latex) or fire-retardant paint *or* cover with new plasterboard (dry-wall or gypsum-board) surface
CLADDING (SIDING)	Timber	Treat as for wood, depending on finish (see above) *or* remove, repair wall surface and redecorate
	Manufactured	Paint *or* remove (see above) *or* cover with lining paper and redecorate

REPAIRING DAMAGE

In the course of preparing the various surfaces of a room for redecoration, you are likely to come across minor (and occasionally major) damage that will have to be put right before you proceed. This section looks at what is involved in restoring walls, ceilings and woodwork in need of more than just a fresh coat of paint.

DAMAGE TO WALLS AND CEILINGS

The most common cause of damage to wall surfaces is accidental impact – a knock from a piece of furniture being moved carelessly or a bump from a child's wheeled toy, for example. On solid walls, the result will range from small dents and cracks in the plaster to larger areas becoming loose, while on timber-framed walls you could end up with a hole in the wall surface.

Ceilings obviously suffer less from impact damage, although carelessly placed feet in the loft have slipped through many a ceiling surface. Two other problems are more common: old age, especially if the ceilings are of lath-and-plaster, and water damage, caused by leaky roofs and leaking plumbing.

PLASTER ON SOLID MASONRY SURFACES

Repair cracks and small-scale damage to plaster on solid masonry using a proprietary filler. Brush out any plaster dust, then use a filling knife or similar tool to undercut the edges of the damaged area to give the filler more purchase. Dampen the surface with water, then press the filler in with the filling knife. Do not try to fill deep holes in one go, or the filler will crack as it dries; work in layers about 3mm (⅛in) thick, allowing each to harden before adding the next one. Build up the repair slightly higher than the surrounding surface so you can sand off the excess with abrasive paper when the filler has set for an invisible repair.

External corners are particularly prone to accidental damage, especially in older homes where metal corner reinforcing beads were not fitted as they are in modern houses. Use an off-cut of wood held against one side of the damaged corner as a former while you fill the defect from the other side. When this has set, smooth over the surface of the patch with a little more filler, and finally sand off the corner to a slightly rounded profile.

Use plaster to patch larger areas of damage. Start by cutting away all loose and unsound plaster with a bolster (wide) chisel and hammer, and undercut the edges of the recess. Then trowel plaster into it to fill it to within about 3mm (⅛in) of the surrounding plaster surface, ruling off any excess with a timber batten (furring strip) pressed against the wall surface and drawn upwards over the repair. Then crosshatch the surface lightly with the corner of the plasterer's trowel and leave it to harden. When it has, smooth on a skim coat of finishing plaster to bring the surface of the repair level with the surrounding wall surface, and polish it smooth with the trowel.

LATH-AND-PLASTER SURFACES

Small-scale damage to lath-and-plaster surfaces usually results in some of the plaster breaking away from the laths. If this occurs but the laths are undamaged, remove all the loose plaster and then patch the damage as for solid walls, forcing plaster against the laths with the trowel so some squeezes between them and forms a secure key for the repair. You can improve the adhesion by brushing some diluted PVA building adhesive onto the laths first. Then complete the repair with a skim of finishing plaster.

More severe damage – a foot through the ceiling, for example – may break some of the laths. If this occurs, cut away the damaged area completely, back to the adjacent joists or wall studs, to form a neat rectangular opening. Then fill this in with a piece of plasterboard (dry wall or gypsum board). (See *Plasterboard Surfaces*, pages 28.)

REPAIRING CRACKS IN PLASTER

1 Where cracks are wider than a hairline, use a cold chisel and club hammer to chop out the sides of the crack, undercutting them slightly.

2 Alternatively, use a small angle grinder. Wear safety goggles as well as gloves when using this tool.

3 Brush out all loose material and dampen the plaster to stop the filler drying out too quickly. Fill the crack or patch just proud of its surroundings, then sand to a smooth finish once the filler has set.

PATCHING PLASTER

1 If an area of plaster sounds hollow when tapped, it has lost its adhesion to the wall and must be chopped out. With plaster on solid masonry walls, do this with a bolster (wide) chisel and a club hammer, then fill as shown opposite.

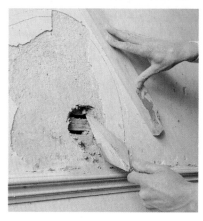

2 If only the finishing coat is damaged, crosshatch it with a cutting knife and then chip the plaster away carefully with a bolster or stripping knife.

3 If old plaster is coming away from wooden laths, chip away the loose plaster with a plasterer's trowel.

4 Brush diluted PVA adhesive onto the laths first to improve the adhesion of the repair.

5 Then fill the hole with plaster, forcing it firmly against the laths so it forms a key between them that will hold the repair in place.

6 Key this layer of plaster by drawing the tip of the trowel or plasterer's float across the nearly-dry plaster to roughen the surface.

7 Complete the repair by applying a skim coat of finishing plaster, making sure it is left flush with the surrounding sound plasterwork.

FILLING PLASTERBOARD (DRY WALL OR GYPSUM BOARD) JOINTS

 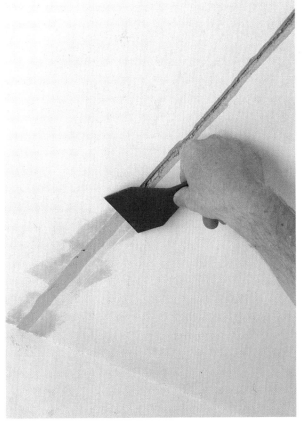

1 If joints open up between ceiling or wall boards, use a sharp cutting knife to rake out the old joint filler and open the joints up.

2 Fill the joints along their length, just proud of the surrounding plaster. When the filler has set, sand the repair down flush with the board surface.

PATCHING PLASTERBOARD (DRY WALL OR GYPSUM BOARD)

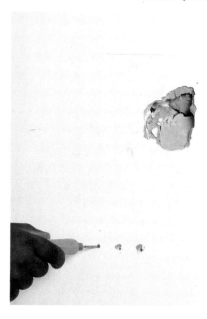

1 If the board is badly holed and cannot be repaired with tape and filler, locate the adjacent frame members with a drill or bradawl.

2 When you have located them, use a sharp cutting knife and a metal straightedge to make horizontal cuts through the board above and below the hole. Then make vertical cuts in line with the frame members.

3 Remove the damaged panel. Make up a screwed framework of wood to fit between the joists or studs. Manoeuvre the frame into place and screw through it into the joists.

4 Cut a piece of replacement board to fit the recess and nail it to the supporting battens. Finish the job by filling the joints all round.

PLASTERBOARD SURFACES

Damaged plasterboard (dry wall or gypsum board) demands differing repair techniques, depending on the extent of the damage. You can fill dents with filler, and disguise small holes with special scrim tape. For holes bigger than 25mm (1in) or so across, use an off-cut of plasterboard to fill the hole. Cut a strip about three times as long as the hole is wide, but a little narrower than its smaller dimension, and drill a hole in the middle. Thread some string through it, butter some filler onto the ends of the strip and feed it in through the hole. Use the string to pull it back flat against the inner face of the wall, where the filler will stick it in place. When this has set, cut off the string and fill the recess with more filler.

To repair larger holes, use a pad (keyhole) saw to cut away the board back to the adjacent joists or wall studs, leaving a neat square or rectangular opening. Then make up a screwed framework of wood to fit between the joists or studs, so that two sides of the frame fit against the joists/studs and the other two sit behind the cut edges of the board. Manoeuvre the frame into place and screw through it into the joists/studs. Then cut a plasterboard patch to fit the hole and nail it into place against the frame. Put scrim tape along the joints, then skim some finishing plaster over the patch to complete the repair. Use this technique to repair large holes in lath-and-plaster walls and ceilings too, after cutting out the damaged laths and plaster.

If you find cracks opening up between the boards of a plasterboard ceiling, fill them with plaster or a proprietary filler. However, if your ceiling is prone to movement, causing the cracks to open up again, refill with a flexible decorators' mastic (caulking). Lastly, you may be unlucky enough to have suffered water damage to a ceiling as a result of a plumbing leak or some structural fault. If plaster is loose or boards are sagging, it is best to pull them down and replace the ceiling surface. However, if the ceiling has survived but is stained, seal the surface with diluted PVA building adhesive or a proprietary stain sealer, otherwise the stain will travel through any subsequent paint finish.

DAMAGE TO WOODWORK

In the course of preparing your woodwork for redecoration, you are certain to come across minor surface blemishes which you can tackle with filler. You may also find more serious faults – mouldings that are split or damaged, loose fixings and the like.

You may be able to repair badly damaged mouldings temporarily with wood filler, but the best long-term solution is to replace them with new wood. Decorative mouldings such as architraves and skirting boards (baseboards) are generally nailed in place – the former to the edges of the door frame, and the latter either to wooden fixing grounds on masonry walls or to the studs and sole plate of timber-framed walls. It is therefore usually a simple matter to prise them away,

although this may cause some localized damage to adjacent plaster surfaces. Picture and dado (chair) rails may also be nailed up, even to solid walls (with cut nails in older homes, masonry nails in newer ones), but are more likely to be screwed into place. If this appears to be the case, try to prise the rail away from the wall enough to allow wedges to be driven in behind it, then cut through the fixing screw with a hacksaw. This is far quicker than trying to locate and clear the hidden screw heads, and a couple of blows with a hammer and punch will quickly drive the screw shank into the wall ready for filling.

Once you have removed the old mouldings, make good any damage and measure up for their replacements. Check that fixing grounds for skirting boards are sound, replacing any

that are split, rotten or damaged by insect attack. Then fit the new mouldings with nails or screws as appropriate. When positioning picture and dado rails, draw a truly horizontal guideline on the wall surface first, then offer up the first length and mark the fixing positions on the wall. Fix one end first, then the other, making the intermediate fixings last of all.

If you find mouldings that are in sound condition but are insecurely fixed, it is a simple matter to add extra fixings – nails in the case of architraves and skirtings, screws and wallplugs for picture and dado rails (especially if the former are to carry heavy pictures). Punch nail heads below the surface of the wood and countersink screw heads deeply, then hide them with filler.

FIXING TIMBER GROUNDS FOR SKIRTING BOARDS (BASEBOARDS)

1 In older homes skirting boards are nailed to timber fixing grounds. If they are rotten, prise them off and fill the holes with mortar.

2 If the grounds are sound, nail on horizontal battens (furring strips) so their outer surfaces are flush with the face of the wall plaster above.

3 Vary the thickness of the packing pieces if necessary to ensure that the battens will support the new boards along their whole length.

4 Add a second batten just above floor level, nailing it direct to the masonry if necessary so it is parallel with the upper batten.

FIXING SKIRTING BOARDS (BASEBOARDS) WITH SCREWS

1 If you are fixing boards to new walls, secure the first length in a corner with screws and wallplugs or masonry nails.

2 Offer up the length of board that will turn the corner and scribe the profile of the first length onto it using a pair of compasses. (Note: this technique requires practice.)

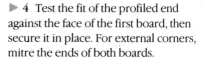

▲ 3 Cut carefully along the scribed line on the second length with a coping saw, then sand the cut end to remove any loose fibres.

▶ 4 Test the fit of the profiled end against the face of the first board, then secure it in place. For external corners, mitre the ends of both boards.

DEALING WITH METALWORK

Unless your home has metal-framed windows, the only metalwork you are likely to have to decorate is plumbing pipework and radiators. Radiators are factory-primed and are then usually decorated with solvent-based paints or with special non-yellowing radiator enamel, while most pipework is bare copper. You do not need to prime this if you want to paint it; just burnish it with wire wool to remove surface oxidation, then apply two coats of solvent-based gloss or satin paint. Always decorate radiators and pipework when cold; heat can be restored once the paint is touch-dry.

If you find signs of rust on ferrous (iron) surfaces, remove it with wire wool or abrasive paper back to bare metal and treat this with zinc phosphate metal primer or a rust inhibitor before repainting it. Watch out for further signs of rust on radiators, which could indicate the presence of a pinhole leak and bigger problems in the future.

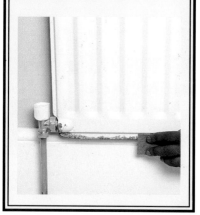

REPLACING ARCHITRAVE SECTIONS

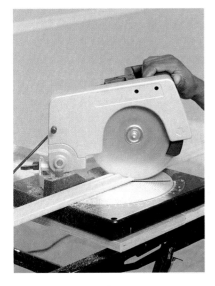

1 You can replace damaged sections of mouldings such as architraves. Remove them using 45° cuts, then measure up and cut the replacement length.

2 Offer up the replacement length to check that it fits and that the 45° cuts are a perfect match. Tap in a fixing nail at each end.

3 Align the length carefully and drive in the two end nails. Then add intermediate nails at about 300mm (12in) intervals.

FIXING DADO (CHAIR) RAILS

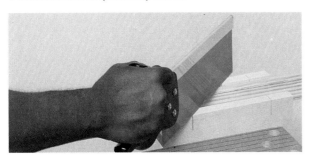

1 Start by cutting 45° mitres on one end of the first two lengths to be fixed in one corner of the room, using a mitre box and tenon saw (backsaw).

2 Drill holes at about 300mm (12in) intervals in each length for the masonry nails that will secure the rail to the wall.

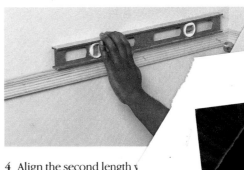

3 Apply PVA adhesive to the rear edge of each length, then fix the first length on the wall in line with a pencilled guideline.

4 Align the second length and check that it is level and drive in nails. Fix subsequent lengths same way.

DECORATING DECISIONS

With all the preparation complete it is time to make some important decisions. You will need to decide on the types of decorating materials you would like to use in various locations, and to make the right choices you will need to consider several factors. For example, you may need a durable finish if decorating a busy through-way such as a hall or a children's play room, and a water-resistant one if decorating a bathroom or kitchen. Your choice of finish may also be limited by the condition of the walls, ceilings and woodwork; and, of course, the cost of materials may also be a deciding factor.

The fun part of redecorating is choosing a new colour scheme, but the wide range of colours and designs available to the home-decorator can make these decisions confusing. However, there are some basic rules of colour and pattern balance that are easy to follow, and once mastered will prevent any costly mistakes.

Plain colours are often the only decoration a room needs, especially if furniture, wallhangings and other accessories provide keynotes of contrasting colour and texture.

DESIGN CONSIDERATIONS

Most home decorators find the whole business of colour scheming quite daunting, which probably explains why paint manufacturers sell more white and magnolia paint than any other colour. Yet it need not be so; all you really need to make a successful choice of colour and pattern is a basic knowledge of the theory of colour and an understanding of how to make colour, pattern and texture work together. Once you have grasped these principles, you will have no trouble putting together colour schemes that are attractive to the eye and pleasant to live with, while making the most of the features of the room concerned.

THE BASICS OF COLOUR THEORY

All colours are mixtures – initially of varying proportions of the three primary colours, red, yellow and blue. Your colour television employs three colour 'guns' to create a picture, and colour printing processes also use the same three primary colours (with the addition of black) to produce every colour under the rainbow.

Picture these three colours as segments of a wheel, and imagine mixing adjacent colours together. Yellow and blue mix to produce green; blue and red make violet; red and yellow make orange. These three are called secondary colours. Add them to the wheel and you have six segments: red, orange, yellow, green, blue and violet. If you then mix adjacent pairs of colours – one primary, one secondary – you end up with the six tertiary colours. The wheel now has twelve segments: red, red-orange, orange, orange-yellow, yellow, yellow-green, green, green-blue, blue, blue-violet, violet and violet-red. These twelve colours, presented in this visual form, are known as the colour wheel, and this is the basic tool for all colour scheming.

HOW COLOURS WORK

The segments of the colour wheel can be divided into two groups. Those from violet round to yellow are regarded as 'advancing' colours, because they make a room look warm and inviting by making the walls appear to advance towards the viewer. This, incidentally, also has the effect of making the room appear smaller.

The other side of the wheel, from yellow-green to blue-violet, consists of 'receding' colours. These make a room seem more spacious – and also cool and potentially unwelcoming to the viewer.

Colours on diametrically opposite sides of the wheel are called complementary colours, and are used in a colour scheme to provide elements of contrast – a vital consideration if your colour schemes are not to appear bland and monotonous to the eye. On the other hand, colours next to each other, or at least in the same part of the colour wheel, provide colour harmony; they will go well together in a colour scheme without clashing.

Yellow is known as an 'advancing' colour, making a room look warm and inviting – the perfect choice for an area with poor natural light, such as a basement living room. Here a hand-painted frieze adds touches of contrasting shades, bringing the colour scheme to life.

COLOUR CONTRAST AND HARMONY

As already mentioned, every colour scheme needs some contrast to make the room stimulating to the eye, and is particularly useful in rooms you use only occasionally – the bathroom or the entrance hall, for example. The drawback is that contrast tends to mark out individual areas of the room very clearly, and so can make it look somewhat uncoordinated unless used with care. Colour harmony works in the opposite way; a harmonious colour scheme is restful on the eye, and helps to blend the various features of the room visually. It is best brought into play for rooms where you tend to spend most of your time, such as sitting rooms and bedrooms. However, too much harmony can be as bad as too much contrast; the latter offends the eye, while the former simply makes it want to close from visual boredom!

The way out of this seeming impasse is to aim for a colour scheme that is basically harmonious, with one group of colours as its main theme, and then to add a little contrast using accessories or other small features in colours complementary to those in your basic colour scheme.

You can create a similar effect of balance by mixing pattern in with your basic plain colours. For example, you could have three painted walls in a room, and decorate the fourth with a patterned wallcovering in a design and colour complementary to the predominant paint colour. Similarly, using a patterned rug on a plain carpet adds visual interest to an otherwise featureless expanse of single colour.

Blue brings a cool, spacious air to any room, especially if the colour is extended to the woodwork too.

COLOUR INTENSITY AND PERSONALITY

You can alter the intensity of any colour on the colour wheel (and of any one of the infinite variety of intermediate shades created by further mixing of adjacent colours) by adding white or black. This produces lighter or darker shades of the original colour, and so widens your colour palette still further.

The three primary colours are regarded as having the highest colour intensity, and so should be used relatively sparingly in the same way as elements of colour contrast are introduced, especially in frequently used rooms. Too much of any of them is simply exhausting on the eye.

Colours have personalities too, which help to determine the sort of atmosphere they give to a room. As mentioned earlier, red and orange shades make a room look warm and inviting, with the red-oranges particularly reminiscent of the fireside. Move towards the yellows and you suggest sunlight, making them a good choice for brightening up rooms with poor natural light. The greens induce a cool and restful feel, so are ideal both for work rooms such as kitchens and also for relaxation areas with an outdoor feel such as conservatories.

Move into the blue area of the colour wheel and you get an impression of spaciousness coupled with an even cooler feel than with the greens. They are a popular choice for kitchens and bathrooms, but should be avoided in north-facing rooms which get little or no direct sunlight. By contrast, the blue-violets give a richly sumptuous look to any room, though they can be somewhat overpowering if over-used.

The pinks are a popular choice for many colour schemes, since they appear warm and welcoming to the eye; they are widely used in bedrooms, bathrooms and nurseries for this reason. Lastly, browns and creams are subdued and comforting too, but need some subtle colour contrast to prevent them from looking dull.

PUTTING THEORY INTO PRACTICE

We have already seen that colour can give a room a distinct atmosphere – warm, cool, restful and so on. It can also be used to alter the room's appearance. You can find out whether you need to do this by looking at the room for which you are planning a new colour scheme, and asking yourself questions such

as these. For example, is the room too high, long and narrow, or square and box-like? Is it well-lit by large, well-placed windows, or is it poorly lit because they are too small or wrongly positioned? Are there a lot of doors which break up the wall area? Does the room appear small and cramped or large and under-used? Are there any particular features of the room that could be emphasized as part of the new colour scheme? Conversely, what about features you would prefer to hide, such as unattractive radiators or exposed pipework? The answers to these questions will help you decide which of the following visual 'tricks' you can employ to alter and improve the room's appearance.

Above: *Green is a cool and restful colour, ideal for the working areas of the home. Link hall, stairs and landing areas with the same colour scheme to achieve harmony.*

Below: *Pink is a warm and welcoming colour – a popular choice for bedrooms.*

ALTERING THE ROOM HEIGHT

One of the simplest colour tricks in the book is to make a high ceiling look lower by decorating it in a dark colour. If it has any decorative mouldings such as a cornice (crown molding) or a ceiling centre, picking these out in white will make them more noticeable, and will make the ceiling appear closer to the eye. You can increase this effect still further by using a floorcovering in a similar colour to the ceiling; the two darker areas, separated by lighter-coloured walls, appear to draw floor and ceiling together and create the illusion of reducing the room height very effectively.

A similar trick involves breaking up the upper reaches of the walls by putting up a frieze or picture rail, and then continuing the dark ceiling colour down the walls to meet it.

Wallcoverings with a strong element of horizontal pattern have the same effect of reducing apparent ceiling height. If the room's windows are large you can echo this approach in your choice of curtain materials. However, use this particular trick sparingly in generously proportioned older houses that retain their original internal features; here a better solution to the problem of high ceilings is to choose furniture that matches the scale of the room. This means avoiding low modern chairs, tables, fire surrounds and the like; instead, select tall chairs and cupboards and a high mantelshelf to maintain the correct scale of the room.

The reverse of the paint and wallcovering tricks can be used to help make a room with a low ceiling appear higher and less claustrophobic. In this case, go for light-coloured or white ceilings, and choose a wallcovering design with a strong vertical emphasis – stripes, for example. This makes the walls appear taller and the ceiling higher.

ALTERING THE ROOM WIDTH

You can use the horizontally patterned wallpaper trick described for altering the room height (left) to make a narrow room appear wider as well as lowering the apparent ceiling level. Reinforce it by laying a floorcovering with a definite linear element running across the width of the room. Alternatively, lay a plain-coloured floorcovering and paint the skirting boards (baseboards) in the same colour to make the floor area look larger than it really is.

The reverse – using strong vertical patterns on the walls and running a linear-patterned floorcovering along the length of the room – will make it appear narrower and deeper than it actually is.

THE EFFECT OF PATTERNS

Remember that the size of pattern motifs on walls can also have an effect on room size. Large patterns make a wall appear smaller, while small patterns have the opposite effect since the shapes make the wall appear to recede.

To alter the appearance of a square and featureless room, throw the colour scheme out of balance by concentrating the eye on just one wall – perhaps with a striking wallcovering to contrast with the remaining plain walls, or by creating framed areas with mouldings to act as a display focus for a large picture or mirror.

The classic way of making a low ceiling appear higher is to use wallcoverings with a strong vertical stripe. Paint the ceiling a light colour to reinforce the effect.

COPING WITH SLOPING CEILINGS

In rooms with sloping ceilings it is often difficult to decide where the walls end and the ceiling starts. With small rooms, the best solution is often to decorate the whole room either with one shade of paint, or with a wallcovering that has a very small random and non-directional pattern which can be taken up one wall, across the ceiling and down the other wall. In larger rooms, one option is to fix a dado rail (chair rail) at window-sill height and hang paper below it and paint above it – ceiling included. Add a frieze or border if you want to highlight the wall–ceiling divide and add a decorative touch to the room. It is generally best to confine wallcoverings with a definite pattern to just the vertical end walls of the room; you will have great difficulty making the pattern match otherwise.

HIDING UGLY FEATURES

Many rooms have features you may want to disguise rather than enhance, and you can often do this by means of clever use of colour and pattern. For example, ugly radiators and pipework can be made less noticeable if they are painted in the same colour as the walls themselves (or in the dominant shade present in the wallcovering if the walls are papered). Chimney breasts recede somewhat if decorated in the same way as the adjacent walls, or if the rear walls of the chimney-breast alcoves are given a different decorative treatment to the rest of the room. Lintels replacing walls in through-room conversions are also best decorated in the same way as the adjacent surfaces, or else can be treated as 'ceiling' if that is coloured rather than white.

Above right: *If you want wallcoverings in rooms with sloping ceilings, use them only on the vertical end walls. Emphasize the wall–ceiling divide with a toning border, if wished.*

Right: *Paint unattractive features such as radiators the same colour as the walls to make them less obtrusive.*

DECORATING OPTIONS

The precise choice of decorating material you make for each room in the house will depend mainly on the look you want to achieve. But there are several other factors you should also take into account.

The first is durability. Obviously the decorations in a house full of young children will have to endure far more day-to-day abuse than those in a retirement cottage, so think carefully about the wear and tear that individual areas of the home are likely to be subjected to.

The second factor is the state of the surface being decorated. If your walls and ceilings are full of lumps, bumps and cracks you will want to choose decorating materials that hide the blemishes. These will also cut down on the amount of preparation needed.

The third factor is ease of redecoration. If you like to give your home a fresh look every couple of years, it is best to choose materials that can be applied quickly and then changed relatively easily without a great deal of laborious stripping and preparation work.

The fourth – and often the overriding – factor is cost. Some decorating materials are very expensive and so will have to be used sparingly – and made to last a long time. They can often be used together with less expensive materials which you can afford to change more regularly.

WALLS AND CEILINGS IN PERFECT CONDITION

The choice is endless; you can use any decorating material you like, subject only to other constraints such as durability, ease of redecoration and cost.

Paint is the perfect low-cost option; some of the more expensive materials you could consider include hand-printed wallpapers, metallic foils, flocks and smooth fabric wallcoverings such as silk or felt.

Hand-printed wallpaper brings a touch of opulence to any room – at a price – but should only be used on wall surfaces in tip-top condition.

WALLS AND CEILINGS IN POOR CONDITION

The best combination of economy and performance is either a relief wallcovering or, in the case of ceilings, a textured finish. Both are relatively inexpensive to use and will hide a multitude of sins. In addition, once up, each can be repainted when a change of colour scheme is desired.

If expense is less important, your options include using wallboards, cladding (siding) or ceramic tiles – the latter only where the wall surface is sound even if it is uneven.

Left: *Painted relief wallcoverings are the perfect cover-up for walls with minor cracks and a few lumps and bumps.*

WALLS AND CEILINGS IN AVERAGE CONDITION

Here your choice widens. If you want a painted finish, the least expensive option is to hang lining paper first and then to paint over it; alternatively you could put up a relief wallcovering instead. If you want pattern rather than flat colour, a printed wallcovering with a textured finish will disguise any slight surface imperfections; choose ordinary paper, a washable or a vinyl according to the degree of durability you want to achieve.

You could also consider a coarse fabric wallcovering such as grasscloth or hessian (burlap). Cork wall tiles are another possibility, but bear in mind that once up they are very difficult to remove when you want a change of colour scheme.

Vinyls, especially ready-pasted ones, are hardwearing and easy to hang. Many collections feature complementary designs.

DURABLE SURFACES

For a durable long-term finish, the best materials to use for walls are, in ascending order of cost, solvent-based (alkyd) paint, painted heavy embossed or relief wallpaper, heavy-duty vinyl wallcoverings, natural or manmade wallboards or cladding (siding), and ceramic tiles. Solvent-based paints can stand far more repeated washing and scrubbing than emulsion (latex) paints, are easy to paint over when you want a change of colour scheme, and can also be used over relief wallcoverings as well as on bare plaster. Vinyl wallcoverings combine a tough surface with relative ease of redecoration. Cladding and tiles are ideal choices for a durable finish that will not be changed regularly.

Washable wallcoverings, while less tough than vinyls, will tolerate sponging (but not scrubbing) and so are an economical alternative in situations where regular redecoration is likely to take place.

WATER-RESISTANT SURFACES

Choose from paint, washable or vinyl wallcoverings, sealed cork tiles, wall cladding (siding) and, at the top of the price range, ceramic tiles. Remember that the last three are all semi-permanent decorations.

EVERLASTING SURFACES

Irrespective of cost, your choices include the really heavy-duty vinyls, painted heavyweight embossed papers, coarse fabrics such as hessian (burlap) and woolstrand wallcoverings, plastic laminates, brick, stone and ceramic tiles and timber cladding (siding) or panelling. Make your choice according to the type of decorative effect you prefer.

QUICK DECORATING

Paint is the obvious first choice, either on plaster or over lining or relief papers, especially if keeping costs down matters. Do not forget the option of using one of the many applied paint effects such as stippling or ragging, all of which can create very attractive decorative effects for relatively little outlay. If you want pattern at low cost, ordinary printed wallpapers are relatively inexpensive and are easy to strip, although hanging them obviously takes longer than repainting would. Vinyl and polyethylene wallcoverings are easy to strip for redecoration, but obviously cost more than ordinary wallpapers.

WOODWORK

Your choices are obviously more limited – essentially to paint or varnish. Use high-gloss finishes on woodwork in perfect condition, and eggshell or satin finishes where the wood surface has a few knocks and blemishes. Varnished finishes tend to show up dirt and fingerprints less readily than paint, and also need redecorating less frequently. Wood stains can help hide stains and blemishes in wood to be given a clear finish. Lastly, do not forget that there are plenty of special paint effects you can use on woodwork as well as on walls.

Opposite above: *Heavy embossed wallcoverings with a coat of solvent-based (alkyd) paint provide a durable, easy-to-clean wall or ceiling surface.*

Opposite below: *Paint is the ideal all-purpose finish for walls and woodwork, especially in 'wet' areas such as bathrooms.*

Right: *The woodwork in a room does not have to be all the same colour; contrasting and complementary colours can help to emphasize unusual features.*

OPTIONS CHECKLIST

FOR WALL/CEILING SURFACES IN PERFECT CONDITION	Paint	Any wallcovering
FOR WALL/CEILING SURFACES IN AVERAGE CONDITION	Lining paper, then paint Relief wallcoverings, then paint Patterned wallcoverings with some surface texture	Coarse-weave fabric wallcoverings Textured finishes
FOR WALL/CEILING SURFACES IN POOR CONDITION	Heavy relief wallcoverings, then paint Heavy-duty 'blown' vinyl wallcoverings	Wallboards or cladding (siding) Textured paint (for ceilings)
QUICK AND INEXPENSIVE WALL/CEILING COVER-UPS	Emulsion (latex) paint Ordinary printed wallpaper	Lining, light relief or woodchip paper, then paint
DURABLE LONG-TERM FINISHES	Solvent-based (alkyd) paint Heavy-duty vinyl wallcoverings Heavily embossed/relief wallcoverings	Wallboards or cladding Ceramic tiles
SPLASHPROOF/WASHABLE FINISHES	Solvent-based paint on walls, ceilings and woodwork Washable or vinyl wallcoverings	Wallboards Ceramic or sealed cork tiles
LUXURY FINISHES	Flock wallcoverings Fabric wallcoverings Hand-printed wallpapers	Hand-painted ceramic tiles Real wood panelling

PAINT

Paint is by far the most widely used home decorating material – every year several million tins in hundreds of different colours are purchased. Choosing the right paint for the job is just as important as selecting the right colour, so it is vital to know which paint is suitable for what purpose. You will also need to know about the best types of brushes and rollers to use for all manner of painting tasks, and exactly how to use them. Some painting jobs seem especially tricky, especially if faced with a multi-surfaced panelled door or a casement window which needs careful painting. This chapter details all the information, know-how and tricks of the trade that will guarantee perfectly painted surfaces every time.

The classic paint partners for interiors are emulsion (latex) for walls, usually in a satin finish and solvent-based (alkyd) paint in a high-gloss finish for woodwork.

TYPES OF PAINT

Paints have evolved and changed a lot over the past few years and the technical jargon printed on the cans can be confusing if you are simply looking for a traditional emulsion (latex) or high-gloss solvent-based paint. However, knowing what is used in paints today and being aware of all the different bases and finishes available will help you to widen your decorating skills and diversify the decorative effects used in the home.

WHAT IS IN THE TIN?

There are three main ingredients in any paint. Perhaps the most important is the **BINDER**, which makes the paint stick to the surface over which it is applied. It is a liquid in the tin, but it dries into a solid but elastic film that resists water, chemicals and physical knocks – in other words, paint protects as well as decorates. The most common binders used to be natural oils such as linseed or

PAINT TYPES

Emulsion (latex) paint, solvent-based (alkyd) paint and speciality tinted glazes are available in every colour imaginable. In addition, emulsion and solvent-based paints are available in three different finishes – high-gloss, satin and matt.

resins like copal; nowadays a whole range of manufactured chemicals is used instead. You often see the name of the binder on the tin – words like polyurethane, vinyl (short for PVA – polyvinyl acetate) and acrylic.

The **PIGMENT** is mixed into the binder to give the paint its colour and covering power. Titanium dioxide gives white paint its brilliance, and adds opacity to coloured paints in conjunction with other coloured pigments and dyes.

The **THINNER** is the third essential ingredient, making the binder pigment mixture runny enough for easy application. It evaporates as the paint film dries, and it is the type of thinner employed that divides paints into the two major classes used in the home. Water-based paints are better known as emulsion or latex paints, and are so-called

because the binder (which will not normally mix with water) is dispersed in it as tiny droplets, in the same way as the fats in milk. The other thinner widely used is a petroleum by-product better known as white (mineral) spirit or turpentine substitute; paints thinned with this are nowadays referred to as solvent-based or alkyd paints, but previous generations knew them as oil paints.

There are lots of other additives in paint – chemical hardeners, drying agents, plasticizers, stabilizers, anti-skinning agents, extenders and so on. Only one is of any particular importance to the consumer; a thixotropic agent (see page 44).

USING NON-DRIP GLOSS

Above: *Non-drip gloss allows you to apply a thicker coat than is possible with traditional liquid gloss paints, so gives better one-coat coverage.*

NON-DRIP PAINTS

Paint is a fairly runny liquid, as many amateur decorators have found to their cost. But today most paints sold for the domestic market contain special additives to give them a jelly-like consistency. Such paints are called thixotropic (a term sometimes seen on the tin) by the makers, but are better known as non-drip paints.

The description is not strictly true. The paint has a firm jelly-like consistency in the tin, but when it is stirred it becomes runny – just like an ordinary paint. If it is then left to stand, it reverts back to a jelly again. This same effect takes place when you actually dip your brush into the paint and start to apply it to a surface. Initially, the jelly-like structure stops the paint from dripping off the brush. Then, as you start to brush it out, the jelly breaks down and allows the paint to flow smoothly onto the painting surface. Stop brushing, and the jelly begins to reform, stopping the paint from running off the surface and forming drip marks.

Apart from the obvious advantage of minimizing drips and runs, non-drip paints have another major advantage. Because they do not run as much as ordinary paints, you can actually apply a thicker coat. This often means that redecorating will involve applying just one fresh coat of paint, rather than the usual two.

WOOD PAINTS

Below, from left to right: *transparent glaze; solvent-based gloss; solvent-based undercoat; solvent-based satin finish; solvent-based paint in matt finish.*

A CHOICE OF FINISH

As paint dries, the finish achieved can be a high-gloss, a silky sheen or a matt (flat or non-reflective) effect. This depends to a certain extent on the binder used, but also on the pigment. Paints that dry to a matt finish contain more pigment than those giving a gloss finish, and also the pigment particles are actually bigger, so therefore the surface film is slightly rough and scatters light falling onto it instead of reflecting it like a mirror.

You can have a high-gloss, satin (medium-gloss) or matt finish with water-based emulsion (latex) paints and with solvent-based (alkyd) gloss. Gloss emulsions are not as hard-wearing as solvent-based gloss, and tend to lose their gloss more quickly. They are very popular in hotter countries where the high temperatures make solvent-based paints dry too quickly. Moreover, they are likely to be more widely used as the dangers of long exposure to evaporating paint solvents become more widely recognized. Matt finishes of both types are also less durable; cleaning produces a slight surface sheen, due to the surface roughness being polished by the cleaning action.

Generally speaking, high-gloss solvent-based paints are used for wood and metal, and matt emulsion paints for walls and ceilings. Paints giving satin or silk finishes can be used on both surfaces – water-based types on walls and solvent-based ones on woodwork – and are particularly good for disguising surface imperfections which a high-gloss finish would exaggerate. Solvent-based paints giving a semi-matt finish are often described as satin gloss, otherwise known in the trade as eggshell.

DURABILITY

Solvent-based (alkyd) paints, especially those with a high-gloss finish, are generally more durable than the emulsion (latex) paints. Satin gloss paint may be worth considering instead of emulsion on walls that need repeated washing – matt emulsion paints tend to develop a noticeable sheen if cleaned regularly.

A CHOICE OF COLOUR

Emulsion and solvent-based paints are available in a huge range of colours, both ready-mixed and from in-store paint tinting machines, so there should be no difficulty in obtaining the exact shade you want. Most manufacturers offer the same shades in both paint types, so you can match or coordinate walls, woodwork and metalwork with ease.

There are two points to remember when selecting paint colours. Firstly, the shade card can only provide an approximation of the final paint colour and should always be viewed in natural daylight, never under fluorescent lighting. Secondly, the freshly-applied paint will look somewhat different to the expected colour: do not be alarmed by this – simply wait until the film has dried.

Some paint manufacturers now offer small 'test' pots of their more popular paint colours, allowing you to decorate a small area before making a final decision on colour. They can certainly help you avoid expensive mistakes in colour scheming.

One last piece of advice: if you are buying your paint from a tinting machine, make sure you buy as much as you will need for the job in one batch – getting a precise colour match from a second batch can be difficult, even from the same machine.

COLOUR RANGE

Below and right: *Paints, whether water- or solvent-based, can be found in a multitude of shades from bright primary colours to neutral tones. In addition the chosen finish can be a high gloss, a soft satin or a flat matt.*

EASE OF USE

Most people find that it is somewhat easier to use emulsions than solvent-based paints, because they seem less 'sticky' and brush out more readily. Avoiding brush marks and getting even coverage is easier with emulsions too. There is very little difference between the types as far as method of application is concerned – both can be put on with brushes, rollers, paint pads, even spray equipment, although rollers are seldom used with solvent-based types because they leave a distinct texture on the paint surface.

The most significant development in paint technology as far as ease of use is concerned is the introduction of 'solid' emulsion. This is an ultra-thixotropic paint sold in its own roller tray (and meant to be applied only with a roller), and it comes closest of all to being a totally non-drip paint.

USING SOLID EMULSION (LATEX) PAINT

1 Solid emulsion is sold packed in its own roller tray. Load the roller sleeve by running it up and down over the paint surface.

2 Move to the ceiling or wall surface and push the roller backwards and forwards across it to distribute the paint evenly.

PAINT COVERAGE

This depends to a large extent on the surface that is being painted, especially as far as walls and ceilings are concerned. Generally, a solvent-based type will cover roughly 10 per cent more than an emulsion – typically about 16 m² per litre (98 ft² per UK pint/81 ft² per US pint) compared with around 14 m² per litre (86 ft² per UK pint/71ft² per US pint) for emulsion paints on smooth surfaces. On rougher surfaces, emulsion coverage can drop to as little as 4 m² per litre (24 ft² per UK pint/20ft² per US pint). Non-drip paints of both types cover about 20 per cent less than their 'runny' counterparts.

Paint type	Coverage		
	m²/l	ft²/UK pt	ft²/US pt
Wood primer*	9–15	55–92	46–76
Aluminium primer	16	98	81
Primer/undercoat*	11	67	56
Metal primer	10	61	51
Stabilizing primer*	6	37	31
Undercoat	11	67	56
Liquid gloss	17	104	87
Non-drip gloss	13	79	66
Eggshell	12	73	61
Matt emulsion (latex)*	12	73	61
Silk emulsion*	14	86	71
Gloss emulsion	14	86	71
Varnish*	16–24	98–147	81–122

* Coverage depends on roughness and porosity of surface

WHICH PRIMER TO CHOOSE

Surface	Primer
Unpainted softwood, manufactured boards	Wood primer, multi-purpose primer or primer/undercoat
Hardwood and resinous softwood	Aluminium wood primer
New plaster, plasterboard (dry wall or gypsum board)	Multi-purpose primer with solvent-based paint, no primer needed with emulsion (latex) paint
Porous or powdery plaster	Stabilizing solution
Distemper	Stabilizing solution
Wallcoverings	No primer with emulsion paint, matt emulsion with solvent-based paint
Iron and steel	Zinc chromate primer
Galvanized iron and steel	Calcium plumbate primer
Aluminium	Zinc chromate or phosphate primer
Copper/brass/lead	No primer needed
Ceramic tiles	Zinc chromate primer

DRYING TIME

Water-based paints dry far more quickly than solvent-based paints – they are usually touch-dry in less than an hour and can be recoated after about four hours. Solvent-based paints are barely touch-dry in that time and should be left to harden for up to 24 hours before applying a second coat. There is a greater chance of dust landing on the slower drying surface and marring the finish.

Some people complain of headaches and nausea when using solvent-based paints and many more find the smell of the drying paint unpleasant. This is due to the evaporation of the solvent, and the only solutions are to ensure good ventilation and to restrict access to the room as far as possible until the paint has completely dried. Proprietary 'smell removers' may help mask the smell, but will not stop the headaches! Because emulsion paint is water-based, there is little smell to worry about.

PRIMERS AND UNDERCOAT

Primers provide a base coat that adheres firmly to the surface being painted, ready for the undercoats and top coats that follow it and build up a complete paint system. On porous materials they seal the surface so that paint does not soak straight into it; on powdery surfaces they act as a binder, while on metal they help to prevent rust. They can also seal in substances that might otherwise ooze out and spoil the paint finish, such as resin in wood or stains in plaster. Use the checklist to select the correct primer for the surface you are decorating.

Use undercoat as an intermediate layer of a solvent-based paint system, to provide a smooth base for the final top coat. Always choose the undercoat in the colour recommended for your chosen top coat.

TEXTURED FINISHES

These are specially thickened products used for decorating walls and ceilings. They are given a random or regular surface texture using a variety of tools once the finish has been applied by brush or roller.

There are two types. The first is a powder which you mix with water (it is also available ready-mixed), while the second is basically thickened emulsion (latex) paint. You can achieve a more pronounced relief with the first type. Both dry white or off-white, and can be painted with emulsion or solvent-based paints for a coloured finish.

VARNISHES AND STAINS

As an alternative to paint, you may prefer to decorate woodwork with a finish that enhances its grain pattern and colour, instead of obscuring it as paint does. Varnishes are the answer.

Varnish is essentially a solvent-based paint without the pigment (although there are now also solvent-free water-based varnishes appearing on the market). The most common type is based on polyurethane resins; these are very hardwearing and ideal for surfaces such as doors and furniture. You can choose a varnish that dries to a high-gloss or to a satin (medium-gloss) finish, depending on the look preferred and also on the condition of the wood (a high gloss will show up imperfections).

If the natural wood colour is weak or you want to colour the surface without obscuring the grain, you can either stain the wood before applying varnish to it, or else use a pigmented varnish known as a coloured sealer which tints the wood without obscuring the grain.

Wood stains are either spirit-based or water-based, and both types come in a wide range of wood shades and primary colours. Different shades of the same stain type can be mixed to achieve the exact colour desired, and both types can be diluted with the appropriate solvent.

OILS AND WAXES

You may also have woodwork in your house that is not finished in paint or varnish but in one of the traditional oils or wax polishes. To maintain a sound finish on these surfaces all you will need is a can of polish and a duster. If you are working on stripped or new wood, these oil and wax finishes make an excellent decorative option.

Perhaps the most satisfying finish for 'good' wood is pure wax. It gives a beautiful glossy sheen, although lots of elbow grease is required to achieve this, and regular refinishing will be needed to keep it in good condition because the surface is relatively soft and marks easily. The best types to use are solid waxes featuring a blend of pure beeswax and carnauba wax.

For a natural seal that is tougher than wax and easier to apply and look after, consider an oiled finish. The best types to use are teak oil or tung oil. The oil is simply applied by cloth or brush and left to penetrate and dry, and the resulting finish is hard, durable and water-resistant.

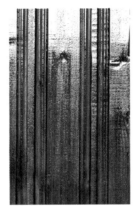

VARNISH/STAIN FINISHES

Above: *Varnishes and wood stains offer a wide range of coloured effects, including (left to right) 'antique-pine' satin varnish, 'rosewood' satin varnish stain and 'black ash' satin water-based varnish stain.*

Below: *Varnish enhances the grain pattern of wood as well as providing a durable, easy-to-clean surface finish. Tinted varnishes are available for a touch of subtle colour.*

TOOLS AND MATERIALS FOR PAINTING

There are three different ways to apply paint to the various surfaces around your home: using a paint brush, a paint roller or a paint pad.

PAINT BRUSHES

A paint brush is by far the most popular tool used by home decorators for painting woodwork and metalwork, and many people prefer them to a roller for painting walls and ceilings too. The best brushes are made with natural pig bristle, but synthetic fibre brushes have become more widespread with some now claimed to give a better finish with water-based paints than the natural-bristle varieties.

A good-quality brush will have thick, relatively long bristles that taper to a thin wedge, while cheap brushes have shorter and fewer bristles (they are bulked out by a thick wooden wedge in the centre of the ferrule securing them to the handle). The ferrule should be non-rusting – a plated finish on most brushes, copper on the more expensive types – and should be securely attached to the handle. This may be of plastic or of painted or varnished wood; choose whichever you find most comfortable to hold.

There are two options (and a compromise) to choose from when buying paint brushes.

The first option – which also gives the best finish – is to buy the best brushes you can afford and to look after them, cleaning them carefully immediately after each use. The second is to buy cheaper brushes and to throw them away after the job is finished. The compromise is to buy brushes with clip-on throw-away heads.

Brush sizes start at 12mm (½in) and go up to 150mm (6in) or more for so-called wall brushes designed for fast coverage of wall and ceiling surfaces. For wall details and woodwork the 12, 25 and 50mm (½, 1 and 2in) sizes are the most useful. For walls and ceilings a 100mm (4in) brush offers the best compromise; it gives reasonably fast coverage, but is not too tiring for the amateur decorator to use for long periods.

You will also find a cutting-in or tapered sash brush useful for painting surfaces such as window glazing bars. The end of the brush is cut off at an angle, making it easier to paint up to an internal corner. There are two common sizes, 12 and 19mm (½ and ¾in).

Lastly, for painting inaccessible areas such as behind radiators, you can buy a crevice brush. This has a short head which is usually attached to a long bendable wire handle. Common sizes are 25, 38 and 50mm (1, 1½ and 2in).

It is well worth investing in a paint kettle, a metal or plastic container into which to decant your paint (via a strainer to remove any dried paint if using an already-opened tin). Tie some thin wire across it between the handle supports; this allows you to 'wipe' excess paint off the brush as you work, and also provides somewhere to rest the wet bristles when necessary.

PAINT ROLLERS

A paint roller is a popular choice for painting walls and ceilings because it offers faster coverage than even a large wall brush. However, it cannot paint right up to internal angles or such obstacles as door architraves. You will need a small paint brush as well for these areas.

The roller consists of a metal frame, usually with a single side arm, with a handle attached to one end and a rotating wire cylinder on the other. The sleeve that actually applies the paint is a rigid tube with fabric bonded to its outer surface; it slides onto this cylinder ready for loading with paint, and is pulled off again for cleaning after the job. There are two common roller sizes, 175 and 225mm (7 and 9in) wide.

The sleeve fabric may be a natural or synthetic fibre, with a short, medium or long

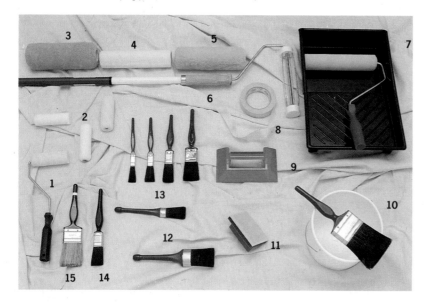

PAINTING EQUIPMENT

You can apply paint with a brush, a roller or a pad. Brushes come in sizes from 12mm (½in) upwards, with a range of handle styles. The bristles may be natural or synthetic, the latter being ideal for water-based paints. Rollers are generally 175mm (7in) or 225mm (9in) wide, with a range of sleeves designed to fit on the rotating roller cage. Mini-rollers are ideal for reaching into awkward corners. Paint pads also come in a range of sizes. You will also need a paint kettle for brush painting and a tray for roller painting.

1 **Mini-roller**
2 **Natural and synthetic sleeves for mini-roller**
3 **Long-pile roller sleeve**
4 **Foam roller sleeve**
5 **Medium-pile roller sleeve**
6 **Roller extension pole**
7 **Roller and tray**
8 **Masking tape**
9 **Paint shield**
10 **Paint kettle**
11 **Paint pad**
12 **Brushes for applying stain and varnish**
13 **Pure bristle brushes in range of sizes**
14 **Cutting-in (or sash) brush**
15 **Synthetic fibre brush for water-based paints**

pile. Use a short pile for smooth surfaces such as plaster, a medium pile for painting relief wallcoverings and the like, and a long pile for applying paint to textured finishes with a high relief. Most medium-priced sleeves are covered in synthetic fibre, which gives excellent results with water-based paints. Mohair sleeves work well with solvent-based (alkyd) paints if you want a completely smooth finish while lambswool sleeves are ideal for applying these paints to relief or highly textured surfaces.

The roller handle may be plastic or wood; again, choose whichever feels most comfortable in the hand. It is worth choosing one to which an extension pole can be attached for painting high ceilings – in stairwells, for example.

To load the roller, you will need a roller tray (unless you are using solid emulsion paint, which is packed in a disposable tray ready for use). This is a shallow plastic or metal container with a sloping ramp at one end. Fill it to about half-way up the ramp, then roll the roller in and out of the paint to coat it evenly ready for use.

You can buy slimline rollers 25 or 50mm (1 or 2in) wide for painting awkward areas such as behind radiators, and there is also a narrow version with a sprung axle and two or three narrow sleeves specially designed for painting pipework.

PAINT PADS

Paint pads consist of a piece of short-pile fabric similar to that used on roller sleeves. It is stuck to a foam backing which is in turn attached to an angled metal or plastic handle. Small types can be used as an alternative to a paint brush, while larger pads are intended for painting walls and ceilings. They are suitable for solvent-based and water-based paints and apply both quickly and evenly. However, they tend to put on a thinner coat of paint than either a brush or roller, so extra coats may be needed to achieve the same covering power.

BEFORE YOU BEGIN
Wherever possible, clear the room of furniture and remove wall-mounted fixtures and fittings. Put dust sheets over any remaining furniture. Protect the floor by taping down overlapping sheets of paper. Affix masking tape all round window panes to keep paint off the glass and ensure a neat paint edge.

Sizes range from around 62 × 50mm (2½ × 2in) for general-purpose work up to 150 × 100mm (6 × 4in) for painting walls and ceilings. You can also buy small slimline pads, often with a bendable handle, for painting inaccessible surfaces such as window shutters.

PAINT SUNDRIES

Apart from tools or equipment for actually applying the paint, you will need dust sheets to protect floors and furniture, masking tape for covering other surfaces to give paint areas a clean edge, plus cleaning solvents to clean up your equipment when the job is done. It is easy to clean emulsion paint from brushes, rollers and pads – simply wash them under a tap. With solvent-based paint, a special cleaner is needed – white (mineral) spirit, paraffin (kerosene) or a proprietary brush cleaner if the paint is fairly fresh, paint remover otherwise. Some modern solvent-based paints contain special additives that allow them to be cleaned off in hot soapy water, but this does not work very well if the paint has hardened – as it does after a long day's decorating. It pays to clean your brush out at regular intervals.

PAINTING TECHNIQUES

If you want your paintwork to have a professional finish, you have to master what is in essence a very simple three-step process: apply the paint, distribute it evenly, then smooth it out. It sounds easy, but plenty can go wrong to spoil things. Poor preparation (see pages 10–31) is the main culprit, but there are others, starting with preparing your paint properly.

APPLYING KNOTTING

On new wood containing resinous knots, apply a special sealer called knotting to prevent the resin from bleeding through the paint film.

PREPARING THE PAINT

Before you even open a tin of paint, wipe the surface of the lid. It may have spent some time on a shop shelf or in your garage, and you do not want accumulated dust and debris getting into the paint.

Next, open the lid properly. With metal lids, use a broad lever rather than the tip of a screwdriver blade, which will deform the lid and make it difficult to replace afterwards. However, a screwdriver is ideal for plastic lids, which have a moulded slot to take the blade tip. Set the lid down inner side up on some newspaper to catch any dribbles.

Now read the instructions on the tin. If it tells you to stir the paint, stir it – with a clean stick, or with a paint mixer attachment in your power drill if you have one. If it says 'Do not stir' (because it is a non-drip paint), you may nevertheless have to stir it if some of the binder has separated out on the surface of the paint. Then leave the paint to stand for a while and regain its gel-like structure.

If you are opening a part-used tin, take care not to allow bits of dried paint to drop into the tin as you open it. If the paint has formed a skin, cut round this carefully with a knife and lift it out.

Whether using a new or an old tin, your next step should always be to pour some paint out into a paint kettle (or a roller tray if roller-painting). Using a paint kettle has two advantages. Firstly, it is lighter and easier to hold than a full tin of paint. Secondly, if you do pick up dust or bits with your brush while painting, you contaminate only a small amount of paint, not the whole tin.

Always use a strainer with old paint to catch any bits. The best material to use for this is some nylon cut from old stockings or tights (pantyhose) and secured over the top of the kettle with an elastic band. When you have finished painting, pour the remaining paint back into the tin – again through a strainer – and replace the tin lid securely.

USING A PAINT BRUSH

The first thing to do with your paint brush is to brush it backwards and forwards across the palm of the hand to remove any dust or loose bristles, especially if it is a new (and cheap) brush. Then make sure you are holding it comfortably. With small brushes – up to about 50mm (2in) wide – you will get better control and find your hands tiring less quickly if you grip the brush at the base of the handle, rather than round the narrow part as you might naturally hold it. Reserve this grip for larger wall brushes, when you will be moving your arm from the elbow rather than from the wrist.

Load your brush by dipping the first third of the bristles into the paint, and draw off excess paint by wiping them lightly against a wire or cord tied across the kettle. Then brush the first stroke of paint onto the surface you are decorating (working parallel with the grain direction when painting wood). Make a second or third stroke alongside the first one if the brush still contains enough paint. Then without reloading the brush, make strokes at right angles to the first ones to distribute the paint evenly over the surface. Finally, smooth off the paint with very light brush strokes parallel to the first stroke.

Reload the brush and repeat the process to paint the adjacent area, linking it to the first with light strokes to keep the paint thickness uniform and the coverage even. Continue this process across the surface. When you reach an edge or corner, brush paint out towards the edge to avoid causing a build-up of paint on the edge itself.

Cutting in – working into an internal angle without getting paint on the adjacent surface – can be tricky. Either use masking tape to protect it or, if you have a steady hand and a good eye, use a cutting-in (sash) brush to apply a neat line of paint into the angle.

APPLYING UNDERCOAT AND GLOSS PAINT

1 Always prime bare wood with a wood primer. Allow to dry and apply an undercoat in the colour recommended for the selected top coat. Also, use an undercoat if repainting in a radically different colour.

2 When the undercoat has dried, rub down with wet-and-dry abrasive paper, used wet, to provide a key for the top coat. If repainting in a similar colour, you will not need an undercoat, but do rub down the surface as described above.

3 Rinse and dry the keyed surface, then start applying the new finish coat, first working along the grain.

4 As you complete adjoining areas, work them together with a series of brush strokes across the grain to get even coverage of the surface.

5 Finish off the newly-painted surface with very light brush strokes parallel with the grain direction for a mirror-like finish.

USING A PAINT ROLLER

Load your roller sleeve with paint by running it down the ramp of the filled roller tray into the paint-well, then back up again. Run it gently up and down the ramp a couple of times to ensure that the paint is evenly distributed in the sleeve, then lift it to the surface to be painted.

Make your first sweep diagonally across the surface to discharge most of the paint. Then roll at a 90 degree angle to the first stroke in one direction to distribute the paint evenly, finishing off with more strokes at right angles to the distributing strokes so the whole area is covered in a criss-cross fashion. Reload the roller and paint the next section, blending the two together as you work.

USING A PAINT PAD

Load a paint pad by dipping just the fabric pile into the paint. Special trays, fitted with a roller at one end, are available; run the pad over the roller to remove excess paint and ensure even distribution in the fabric. Then apply the paint to the surface in adjacent, just overlapping, bands, with further strokes at right angles to the originals if necessary to get uniform coverage. On wood, finish off with final light strokes in line with the grain.

ROLLERING TECHNIQUE

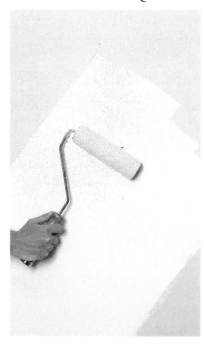

1 You can apply paint to wall and ceiling surfaces using a roller instead of a brush. Start with diagonal passes in one direction.

2 Then run the roller backwards and forwards in passes at right angles to the first ones to distribute the paint evenly and ensure a good coverage.

USING AN EXTENSION POLE
If you have high walls or ceilings to paint, choose a roller that can be fitted with an extension pole to avoid the need for ladders or steps.

PAINTING DOORS

Start by removing the door handles and any other attachments such as hooks or nameplates. Paint the door edges first of all: if opposite faces of the door will be finished in different colours, the convention is to paint the hinged edge to match the closing face of the door (the one that closes against the stop beads), and to paint the handle edge to match the opening face.

When painting a flush door, visually divide the door up into eight squares, and start at the top painting one square at a time. As you work across and then downwards, blend each area in with its neighbours and take care to avoid runs at the edges.

With panelled doors, paint the recessed panels and their mouldings first, then tackle the horizontal top, middle and bottom rails before painting the vertical centre rail and the stiles to finish.

With glazed doors, paint the glazing bars first, using a small cutting-in (or sash) brush; then switch to a larger brush to complete the rails and stiles.

When you have finished, wedge the door wide open and put up a 'Wet paint' sign nearby. Keep pets out of the area.

DOOR FRAMES AND SKIRTING BOARDS (BASEBOARDS)

It is a good idea to paint door frames the day after painting the door; otherwise someone is bound to brush against one while trying to avoid the other. If the paintwork is a different colour in an adjoining room, change colours at the stop bead; use the colour of the opening face of the door on the bead surface against which the door closes, and the closing face colour on the rest of the bead. Paint the rest of the frame and the architrave to match the colour of the adjacent door face.

With skirting boards, the main problem is keeping paint off the wall above and the floor below. Use masking tape on walls and smooth floorcoverings, and tuck a plastic paint shield or lengths of cardboard into the gap between carpet and board as you apply the paint.

PANELLED DOOR

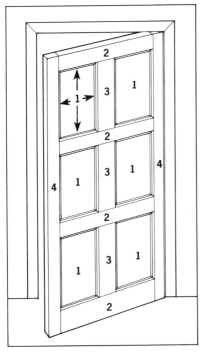

1 PANELS AND MOULDINGS
2 RAILS
3 VERTICAL RAIL
4 STILES

PAINTING DOORS

Paint a flush door by dividing each face into eight imaginary squares, and paint each in turn. On glazed and panelled doors, follow the numbered sequences shown below.

GLASS DOOR

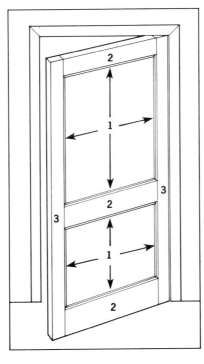

1 GLAZING MOULDINGS
2 RAILS
3 STILES

FLUSH DOOR

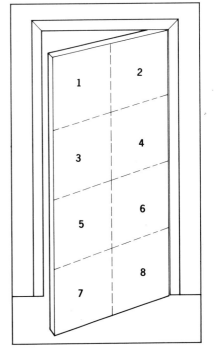

WINDOWS

Whatever type of window you are painting, start with the glazing bars and mouldings round the panes; you might as well get the most difficult part over with first. Either use masking tape on the glass to give a clean paint edge, or use a cutting-in brush and a steady hand. Leave masking tape in place until the paint is just touch-dry.

With opening casement windows, complete the inner faces of the opening casements and toplights next, then do their hinged edges. It will be easier, access permitting, to paint the other casement edges and toplight edges from outside the house. Paint the fixed casement following the same sequence, then complete the job by painting the frame and sill.

Sash windows are rather more difficult to paint, as you have to move the sashes up and down to reach the various parts of the window, and it is physically impossible to paint some of them without actually removing the sashes from the frame. Start by pushing the bottom sash right up and pulling down the top sash so you can paint its lower half. Paint the exposed parts of the frame sides with the sashes in this position, and leave them there until the paint is touch-dry. Then reverse the sash positions so you can paint the top part of the top sash, plus the exposed parts of the frame sides, before painting the bottom sash and finally the frame surround. (See the diagrams, right, for more details.)

PAINTING WINDOWS

With casement windows, tackle the fiddly bits such as the glazing bars first. Then paint the opening lights and casements next, finishing off with the main frame.

Paint sash windows in two sessions, starting with the sashes reversed. Follow the numbered sequence shown in the diagrams.

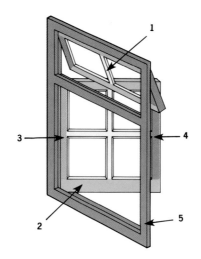

CASEMENT WINDOW

1 GLAZING BARS AND MOULDINGS
2 UPPER AND LOWER RAILS
3 HINGE STILE AND EDGE
4 MEETING STILE
5 FRAME

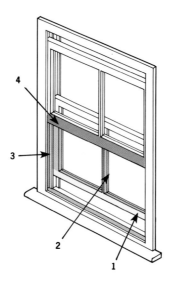

SASH WINDOW

1 LOWER RAIL AND MEETING EDGE (OUTER SASH)
2 STILES UP TO CROSS RAILS (OUTER SASH)
3 LOWER HALF OF SASH RUNNERS AND MEETING EDGE
4 LOWER RAIL AND UNDERSIDE (INNER SASH)

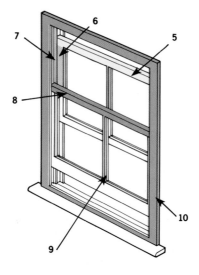

5 UPPER RAIL AND MEETING EDGE (OUTER SASH)
6 REMAINDER OF STILES (OUTER SASH)
7 UPPER HALF OF SASH RUNNERS AND MEETING EDGE
8 UPPER RAIL AND LOCK EDGE (INNER SASH)
9 STILES (INNER SASH)
10 FRAME SURROUND

WALLS AND CEILINGS

Divide walls and ceilings up into imaginary
squares, and simply paint your way across the
surface, joining up adjacent squares as you
proceed. If painting bare plaster, first apply a
coat of diluted emulsion (latex) paint to prime
the surface. When using a roller, brush-paint
a 50mm (2in) wide strip all round the
perimeter of the surface first. You can get
special paint pads with small edge rollers
which enable you to paint neatly into internal
angles simply by running the wheeled edge
along the adjacent surface.

Do not worry if a rash of blisters appears
when you are painting over papered walls.
These will in most cases flatten and
disappear as the paint dries out.

PAINTING WALLS WITH A ROLLER

1 If you are painting new plaster, seal it
first with diluted emulsion (latex) paint
to reduce the porosity and stop the new
paint from being absorbed too quickly.

2 Since the roller will not reach right
into internal angles, paint these in with
a paint brush before starting to use the
roller.

3 Load the roller in your roller tray,
making sure the paint is evenly
distributed, then start rolling the paint
onto the wall surface.

4 Roll the paint on in a series of criss-
crossing strokes for even coverage,
blending each painted area into its
neighbours.

PAINTING WALLS WITH A BRUSH

1 If you are using a brush to paint walls and ceilings, first apply the paint with a loaded brush in a series of overlapping parallel strokes.

2 Then distribute the paint evenly across the surface with brush strokes made crosswise to the original direction of working.

3 Finish off by brushing the paint out with a further series of lighter strokes made in the same direction as the original application strokes.

Paint is a quick, easy and cost-effective means of decorating walls. Add interest to plain walls by using a contrasting colour to accentuate the wall/ceiling divide. Use the contrasting colour for the woodwork, too, for a simple but harmonious decorating scheme.

USING VARNISH AND WOOD STAIN

Apply varnish and coloured sealers as you would paint. If you are varnishing bare wood, thin the first coat slightly with the relevant thinner so it soaks well into the wood and provides a good key for subsequent coats. Apply it with a clean, lint-free cloth, working it well in along the grain. Leave to dry, then sand it down with very fine grade abrasive paper and wipe it over with a tack rag or a cloth moistened with white (mineral) spirit to remove the dust. Brush on an undiluted second coat, allow to dry, then sand and wipe again before applying the third and final coat.

If you are using a wood stain to colour new or stripped wood, experiment first on an unobtrusive part of the surface to obtain the shade and depth of colour you want. Then apply the stain with either a pad of lint-free cloth or a brush, working along the grain and taking care that adjacent bands just touch with no noticeable overlap which will dry darker than the rest of the surface. Leave to dry, then sand the surface very, very lightly to remove any wood fibres raised during the staining process (a common occurrence with water-based stains).

APPLYING VARNISH

First prime bare wood with a coat of varnish diluted with thinner, applied with a lint-free cloth. Then brush on an undiluted second coat, leave to dry, then sand down. Finally, apply the third and last coat of varnish.

Stained and varnished woodwork has a natural beauty that no paint finish can quite match.

PAINTING OTHER SURFACES

Most people have a fair idea of how to go about painting walls, ceilings and woodwork (even if their technique leaves something to be desired). But there are other surface materials – especially metals and plastics – that require a knowledge of the correct procedure if you are to get results that will look good and last reasonably well.

Whatever surface you are decorating, there are the same basic guidelines to follow. The first is to make good any defects, which includes removing unwanted surface encrustations such as rust on iron and steel and oxidation on copper or aluminium. The second is to clean the surface down thoroughly, to remove dirt and grease. The third is to provide the right base coat – usually a primer of some sort – to give subsequent layers of paint the best possible chance of sticking properly; most paint defects are caused by adhesion failure. Precise details vary from material to material, so perhaps the best way to deal with the subject is to look at the various surfaces you are likely to encounter. In each case you will find details of what products and tools to use, and any special tips that will help make the job easier.

METAL WINDOWS

Metal frames in older houses will have been made from galvanized steel, and if the galvanizing is damaged rust will attack the exposed steel and can spread beneath the surface layer at great speed. Wire-brush the affected areas back to bare metal and spot-prime with calcium plumbate primer before repainting with undercoat and topcoat. In future, treat any rust spots as soon as they appear to avoid widespread damage.

Anodized aluminium windows are also attacked by the elements, but in this case a white or grey surface layer of aluminium oxide is formed on the metal surface. Once this has happened no further deterioration takes place. Clean off the oxide with fine emery cloth or wet-and-dry abrasive paper, using white (mineral) spirit as the lubricant; you can then either leave the metal bare or paint it directly with two coats of solvent-based paint.

PAINTING METAL

Once you have removed any traces of rust from iron and steel surfaces, apply a metal primer or use a one-coat rust-inhibiting paint.

OTHER INTERIOR METALWORK

Most interior metalwork – radiators, for example – arrives already primed, so all you have to do is apply undercoat and topcoat in your chosen colour. Tackle localized rust spots first, as for galvanized steel windows.

Copper should be cleaned to a bright finish with wire wool, emery cloth or wet-and-dry abrasive paper, and must also be degreased with white spirit. Undercoat and gloss or eggshell topcoat can then be applied directly.

Other metals such as brass can be left bare (and allowed to tarnish naturally, or else kept bright with a coat of clear lacquer), or may be painted directly as for copper.

PLASTIC SURFACES

Any plastic surface, whether it is a waste-pipe, a window frame or the melamine surface on kitchen cupboards, can be overpainted if it has become yellowed or stained, or for a change of colour scheme. Start by washing the surface down thoroughly with sugar soap or detergent; then sand the surface lightly with wet-and-dry abrasive paper to provide a key for the paint film, and wipe over with white spirit. Finally, apply one or two coats of solvent-based gloss or eggshell paint.

TILED SURFACES

Ceramic tiles that have begun to show signs of age – crazed glaze, dirty grout lines and so on – can be given an inexpensive facelift with a coat of gloss or eggshell paint. Wash down and degrease the surface thoroughly, allow it to dry, then apply a coat of zinc chromate primer followed by an undercoat and one or two topcoats.

Cork tiles can also be overpainted, although only the dense, smooth-surface types take paint successfully. Use emulsion paint, thinning the first coat slightly and then applying two full-strength coats on top. For open-textured tiles you will get better results by hanging lining paper over the tiles first.

TEXTURED FINISHES

Textured surfaces, especially the more deeply sculpted ceiling finishes, are particularly difficult to redecorate successfully. For a start, preparation is made more difficult by the surface relief; using a soft-bristled brush is really the only way to shift dirt, nicotine stains and the like. Once this has been done, wipe over the surface with clean water and leave to dry. Repaint with a long-pile roller which will work the paint into the crevices far more quickly than a brush.

Above right: Use solvent-based (alkyd) paints – gloss or eggshell – for painting pipes, radiators and other indoor metalwork. Remove or treat any traces of rust first, and prime any exposed bare metal.

Below and right: Transform plain white ceramic tiles using a simple repeat stencil motif and either ceramic or eggshell paint. The effect can be stunning.

SPECIAL PAINT EFFECTS

Painted walls and woodwork need not be dull and boring – there are lots of special effects you can use to liven up anything from small areas of wood moulding, such as dado (chair) rails to larger expanses such as wall panelling or walls and ceilings. They are all inexpensive to create, and with a little patience and practice quite stunning results can be achieved.

The more simple decorative effects described here involve the use of broken colour. Various techniques are used to apply a second colour over a

different-coloured basecoat so that the latter still shows through, creating a pleasing two-colour effect. As with all decorating tasks, careful preparation is the first vital step.

SURFACE PREPARATION

If the surface to be decorated is new and has no surface finish, simply sand it down and apply a wood primer and undercoat to wood, a coat of emulsion (latex) to walls. If it is already painted or varnished and the finish is sound, sand the surface down lightly to improve the adhesion of the new finish and

attend to any surface blemishes; no further preparation is needed for painted surfaces, but varnished wood will benefit from an undercoat to help obliterate the grain. If the wood has been wax-polished, strip off all traces of the polish with white (mineral) spirit and fine-grade steel wool.

EQUIPMENT

You need little in the way of equipment to achieve some of the most attractive special paint effects. Shown here are a natural marine sponge, a stippling brush, rags for ragging-on and brushes for dragging.

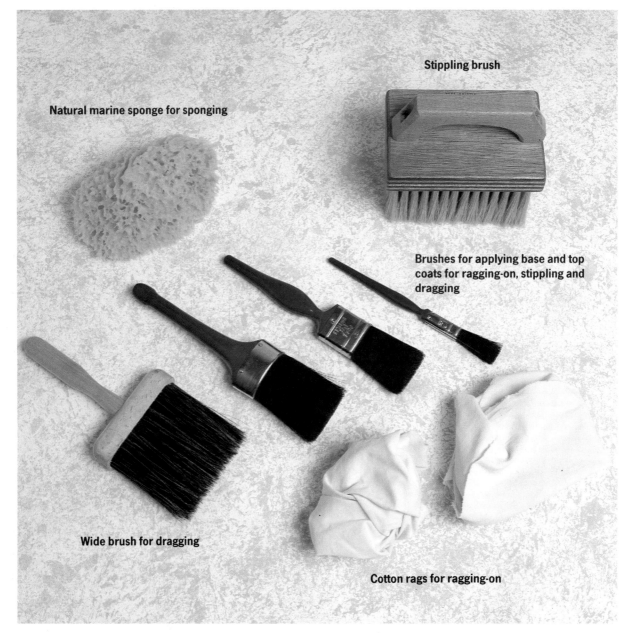

Stippling brush

Natural marine sponge for sponging

Brushes for applying base and top coats for ragging-on, stippling and dragging

Wide brush for dragging

Cotton rags for ragging-on

Right: *Rag-rolling creates a very delicate two-colour finish resembling crushed silk.*

Below: *Sponging is one of the easiest two-colour effects you can apply, but you must use a natural marine sponge.*

CHOOSING THE EFFECT

To help you decide which effect to choose, here is a summary of some of the most popular and easy-to-master techniques.

Sponging involves using a piece of sponge to dab irregular patches of colour over a contrasting basecoat.

Stippling with a special stippling brush gives a plain finish an attractive mottled effect, and is often used to obliterate brush marks before applying another effect over the top.

Ragging involves using pads or rolls of crumpled-up cotton rag or other fabric to apply a random second colour to the surface. Using a pad gives a finish similar to sponging, while rag-rolling creates an effect resembling crushed silk.

Bag graining gives a rather finer textured finish than rag-rolling – more like crushed velvet – and is created by pressing a polythene (plastic) bag filled with crumpled rags onto the wet paint surface.

Dragging involves drawing a dry brush over the wet paint surface to produce parallel lines of colour with the base coat showing through the topcoat. This works only on plain, flat surfaces.

SPONGING

Sponging gives an attractive 'informal' finish to the surface, especially if the base and topcoat colours are similar in shade. On wood, the best material to use for the basecoat is eggshell paint, with thinned eggshell for the topcoat. However, there is no reason why you should not use ordinary emulsion (latex) paint instead, as you would when sponging walls. The only equipment you need is a small bowl and a rounded piece of real marine sponge. Never use a synthetic sponge – it will not work!

Start by applying the basecoat evenly, then leave this to dry. Next pour a little topcoat paint into the bowl, and thin it slightly with white (mineral) spirit if using eggshell paint, or water if working with emulsion paint.

While you are doing this, leave the sponge to soak in water until it expands to its full size. Then squeeze it out well and dab it lightly into the thinned paint – you do not want to pick up too much at one time. It is a good idea to have some scrap paper such as lining paper handy so you can test the effect of the sponge print by dabbing on paint with differing amounts of hand pressure. When you are happy with the look, you can start work on the surface you are decorating.

Simply start at one edge and work over the whole surface, dabbing paint on lightly but evenly and refilling the sponge as necessary. Do not worry if you do not achieve a completely even effect at the first attempt; simply let this coat dry, and then sponge on some more paint over the 'weak' areas. The one thing not to do is to try to add more paint over areas that are still wet, because you will simply smudge the first coat and destroy the speckled effect.

Sponging, as already mentioned, usually works best if the colours used are similar in shade, but you can experiment with combinations of stronger or sharply contrasting colours if you wish.

SPONGING TECHNIQUE

1 After applying the flat base colour, use the sponge to dab on random blotches of the first paint colour.

2 When the first application has dried, deepen the effect by sponging on more paint, filling in any areas that appear light.

3 Again allow this application to dry, then, if wished, sponge on a second colour to create an attractive multi-hued finish.

4 The finished surface, if wished, can be given a coat of clear glaze to enhance the colours and also to improve its durability.

STIPPLING

Stippling is one of the easiest effects to achieve, and creates a finely textured finish that is very easy on the eye. To create it, all you need is a special stippling brush with a head measuring about 100 × 75mm (4 × 3in). The head consists of a bed of fine bristle, cut off square, so that when the brush is used to 'hit' the paint surface all the bristles make contact. If you cannot find such a brush, you can experiment with a clothes brush or even an old-fashioned hairbrush; modern-shaped brushes are ineffective.

Simply brush the diluted topcoat over the dry basecoat, and then immediately stipple the wet film so the base colour just shows through. Make sure the bristles hit the wall squarely, otherwise the effect will smudge.

STIPPLING TECHNIQUE

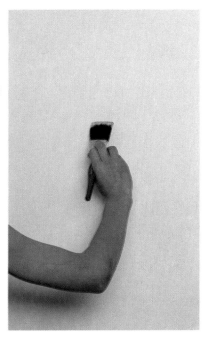

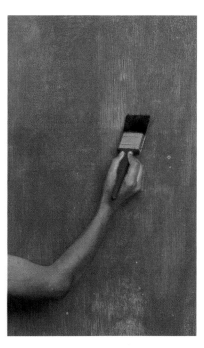

1 Again, start by brushing an even basecoat on to the surface to be decorated, and allow it to dry thoroughly before proceeding.

2 Then brush on the colour to be stippled. Thin it slightly if necessary to get a more open decorative effect.

3 Use the stippling brush flat on to the surface to create the stippled effect, working down and across the surface with an overlapping action.

RAGGING TECHNIQUE

◀ **1** Apply the topcoat over the dry basecoat, brushing it out evenly and laying off the paint with light finishing strokes.

▶ **2** Take a piece of clean, dry, lint-free rag and crumple it up into a ball with plenty of surface creases to give an interesting pattern.

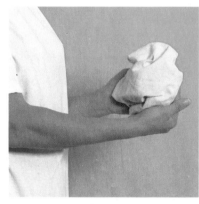

◀ **3** Simply press the crumpled ball of cloth against the wet paint surface, twisting and turning the rag as you work across the surface.

▶ **4** The finished surface. If areas look light, let the paint dry and then rag on some more colour to get an even overall effect.

RAGGING

There are actually two separate ragging techniques, known as rag-rolling (see below) and ragging-on. Ragging-on is a similar technique to sponging, the difference being that a small piece of bunched-up rag is used to apply the topcoat instead of a sponge. Different materials will give different effects, and you can alter the texture of the finish by varying the bunching of the rag pad. Experimenting is once again essential before you actually start work.

Apply the basecoat as before, then simply dip your bunched-up rag into the paint and dab it onto the surface with a light touch. As with sponging, do not try to go over areas that are 'light' in colour while the paint is wet. Instead let it dry and then rag on more colour where necessary. Thin the topcoat to produce a softer print.

Rag-rolling involves rolling a 'sausage' of bunched-up rag over the wet topcoat to create the broken-colour effect. Because of the nature of the technique, it works best on flat surfaces – the rag roll would be awkward to handle on curved or moulded surfaces.

Soft cotton rags are best for this technique, cut into squares. You will need a good supply since they soon become saturated in paint and less effective at creating the pattern. Soak each rag in white (mineral) spirit first, and squeeze it out well; this helps prevent it from clogging with paint.

Apply a smallish area of thinned topcoat to the surface being decorated. Then roll up the rag into a sausage shape and roll it across the paint surface, trying to avoid skids. Keep changing direction, and re-fold the rag from time to time, to ensure the pattern does not look too repetitive. Carry on area by area, changing rags as necessary until you have an even and uniform finish.

BAG-GRAINING

This is a very simple technique that produces a texture similar to rag-rolling, but rather more delicate. It is achieved by texturing the wet topcoat with a polythene (plastic) bag tightly packed with screwed-up rags. You simply brush the well-thinned topcoat on over your basecoat, again treating a smallish area at a time, and then press the bag lightly onto the wet paint film. Make sure that successive dabs overlap each other slightly to create an even, crinkly finish that allows the basecoat to show through. Wipe excess paint off the bag if it begins to build up.

DRAGGING

This is the last of the broken-colour effects, and one of the more difficult to carry off. It involves dragging the bristles of a dry brush over the wet paint to produce regular parallel lines on the surface, so requires a steady hand and a light touch – definitely a technique to practise first. The other problem is that if ordinary paint is used, the brush strokes tend to encourage the paint to flow into an even film, hiding the basecoat. You will get better results using scumble glaze, a transparent or white medium, which you colour with universal stainers or artists' oil paints to the colour you want. The advantage of scumble is that it is slow-drying and stays put instead of running into a smooth layer when the dry brush is drawn over it. Scumble glaze is available from some specialist paint shops. If you don't have an outlet near you, try artists' suppliers.

Thin the scumble glaze with an equal amount of white (mineral) spirit in a paint kettle. Then mix stainer or artists' oil paint with a little glaze and add this to the thinned scumble in your kettle, stirring well. Test the colour, and add more stainer, if necessary, to get the desired shade.

Brush the glaze on over your basecoat, finishing off with brush strokes parallel to the direction you intend your dragging to run so you do not leave any transverse brush marks. Now draw your dragging brush – a paper-hanging brush is ideal for this – lightly across the surface. Overlap successive strokes for a regular striped effect.

DRAGGING TECHNIQUE

1 Apply an even basecoat as before, then brush on a generous coat of the second (graining) colour with an ordinary paint brush.

2 Draw a dry long-bristled brush over the graining colour in a series of parallel sweeps to allow the basecoat to show through.

3 As the graining brush begins to become clogged with the topcoat, wipe off excess paint with a dry cloth before continuing.

WALLCOVERINGS

Choosing a wallcovering is not just a matter of selecting an attractive colour or pattern, there are many other factors involved too. For example, you may choose a plain or textured paper specifically designed to be painted over, or a heavily embossed one to use on a bumpy ceiling to hide all the defects. You may be looking for wallcoverings that can be washed or even scrubbed down, or alternatively a high-quality printed paper or special fabric covering for the 'best' room in the house. There are many wallcoverings available for every need and all the choices are detailed here. In addition, this chapter lists the paperhanging equipment you will need and, most importantly, carefully describes techniques for papering walls, ceilings, alcoves and recesses and for papering round tricky obstacles such as wall lights, radiators and ceiling fixtures.

There is almost a limitless choice of printed wallcovering designs – a tribute to the ingenuity of today's designers.

TYPES OF WALLCOVERING

Wallcoverings can give a room something that paint never can: pattern. But there is more to getting the right effect than just choosing a design you like. You also need to take the shape and style of the room into account. For example, large motifs need plain uninterrupted walls where they can be seen to advantage, while smaller designs are most suitable in rooms with lots of features such as alcoves, window recesses and sloping ceilings. Similarly, designs with a strong vertical theme will be difficult to hang in rooms where the walls are out of alignment. So bear these points in mind when making your initial choice.

Of course, you may prefer to use wallcoverings to provide texture rather than design, by choosing something you can paint over once it has been hung. Using 'whites', as these wallcoverings are known in the trade, is also a good way of disguising walls in less-than-perfect condition.

WALLCOVERINGS TO PAINT OVER

The idea of hanging a wallcovering and then painting over it may sound like making two jobs out of one. It certainly adds to the time the job takes the first time you do it, but you recoup that in the future when redecorating means simply applying another coat of paint.

LINING PAPER

This is not really meant to be used as a wallcovering; its main purpose is to provide a smooth surface for hanging other wallcoverings. However, it is a cheap way of covering up plaster that is full of hairline cracks – although it will not hide major lumps and bumps. Look for the extra-white grade, which is designed for overpainting; other grades have a somewhat hairy surface that does not take paint so well.

WOODCHIP PAPER

A coarse pulpy paper with small chips of wood embedded in it, once painted woodchip has the texture of oatmeal. It is very good at hiding defects in walls and ceilings, and when it has been overpainted a few times it is fairly tough too (when first hung and painted, knocks tend to pull away some of the larger chips). There are several weights available, with the heavier varieties having

the coarser chips. Lightweight types can be tricky to hang because they are rather fragile when wet, but at least tears can simply be pasted back into place.

RELIEF WALLCOVERINGS

These types have a surface carrying random or regular embossed designs, and may be made from paper, cotton fibres or vinyl on a paper backing. Those with a pattern repeat mean you can have 'design' with your colour, and all are excellent at disguising poor surfaces. Care needs to be taken when hanging the cheaper, lighter types, because over-soaking and careless handling can flatten the embossing irreversibly. However, cotton and vinyl types are virtually indestructible, and the vinyl types have the added advantage of being easy to strip – the vinyl surface (plus paint layers) can simply be peeled off dry, just like any other vinyl.

Heavily-embossed relief wallcoverings are immensely hardwearing and are often used to decorate wall surfaces between dado (chair) rails and skirtings (baseboards).

There is also a heavy-duty relief wallcovering made from linseed oil and fillers hardened like putty and formed into thin sheets. It comes in a wide range of heavily embossed decorative effects, is hung with special adhesive and needs overpainting with gloss or eggshell paint. It is extremely durable, but once hung it is difficult to remove, as anyone finding it in an old house will testify. It is also hard to find except from specialist outlets.

TYPES OF WALLCOVERING

*There is a wider choice of colour, pattern
and design available in wallcoverings than
in any other decorating material. You can
often also obtain matching fabrics and
borders for complete colour coordination.*

1 **Lining paper**
2 **Vinyl**
3 **Flock paper**
4 **Small-patterned printed paper**
5 **Hand-printed paper**
6 **Relief/embossed paper**
7 **Wallpaper borders**
8 **Large-patterned printed paper**
9 **Ready-pasted vinyl**
10 **Printed paper**
11 **Grasscloth**
12 **Natural hessian (burlap) paper-
    backed fabric**
13 **Printed fabric**
14 **Woolstrand**
15 **Metallic foils**

ROLL SIZES

Most wallcoverings, including 'whites' and
washables, come in standard-size rolls
10.05m (33ft) long and 520mm (20½in)
wide (or 24ft by 18in in North America).
You may be able to buy longer rolls from
some outlets. Of the fabric papers, hessian
(burlap) is available in standard lengths,
but the others – being extremely expensive –
are usually sold by the metre/yard for
decorating or highlighting small areas such
as alcoves or chimney breasts.
  If the wallcovering is intended for
painting, remember that for every roll you
will need about two-thirds of a litre (about
1 pint) of paint to apply two coats,
so do not forget to add this cost to your
decorating budget.

1

2

3

4

5

10

10

9

8

6

7

WALLCOVERINGS TO WEAR WELL

If you want your wallcoverings to cope with steam, water splashes, sticky fingers and the like, you will need a surface that is easy to keep clean. The painted wallcoverings described in detail on page 67 can be sponged down, of course, and can be given a new coat of paint if the surface becomes too soiled. However, wallcoverings with a plastic surface are both more stain-resistant and easier to keep clean.

WASHABLE WALLPAPER

This is a printed paper which has been given a thin clear plastic coating over the top to make it water- and stain-resistant. This means it can be sponged down, but you should not use any sort of abrasive cleaner or try to scrub the surface. It is a good choice for rooms that get moderate wear, but can be difficult to remove when you want to redecorate – you really need a steam stripper to get it off quickly.

VINYL WALLCOVERINGS

These differ from washable wallpapers in that the design is actually printed onto (and fused into) a plastic film, which is then paper-backed to make it easy to hang. Consequently they are much tougher than washables, and can actually be scrubbed if necessary (so long as you take care near seams and edges). Their other big advantage is that they are easy to strip, since the vinyl layer can be peeled off dry.

FOAMED VINYL WALLCOVERINGS

These differ from ordinary vinyls in that they have a much thicker plastic film, since the plastic is aerated during manufacture. The surface can be heavily textured, or embossed to resemble materials such as tiles and woodgrains. They are useful in rooms prone to light condensation, since the plastic film is a moderate insulator – often enough to prevent condensation from forming.

FOAMED POLYETHYLENE WALLCOVERINGS

All-plastic wallcoverings, these carry a printed design and occasionally a light surface texture. This type of wallcovering is also unusual in that it is hung direct from the roll – you paste the wall, not the wallcovering. It can be washed, but may tear if subjected to knocks and scuffing.

WALLCOVERINGS TO LOOK AT

If you are not unduly worried about how well your wallcoverings will wear or cope with dampness and condensation, you can choose purely on looks – and price.

PRINTED WALLPAPER

Wallpaper with a printed design may also be embossed or textured. You can usually sponge the surface lightly to remove marks – check on the label before you hang it. It is easy to hang and easy to strip, so is an ideal choice if you like to redecorate regularly. Remember that hand-printed varieties can be very expensive.

FLOCK WALLPAPERS

Either printed wallpapers or paper-backed vinyls, flocks are distinguished by a design consisting partially of a raised fibre pile – usually fine wool or silk on paper types, synthetic fibres on vinyls. The latter are extremely hardwearing, combining a luxury look with a scrubbable surface, but paper types are fairly fragile – they also need careful hanging to keep paste off the pile.

Vinyl is the all-purpose wallcovering of today. It is tough, easy to hang (especially if ready-pasted), easy to strip and available in a huge range of designs.

METALLIC FOILS

Usually printed with bold, shiny patterns, the metallized plastic surface of these wallcoverings is bonded to a paper backing. However, these wallcoverings are very fine and this combined with the highly reflective surface makes them suitable only for walls in perfect condition.

PAPER-BACKED FABRICS

Fabrics such as hessian (burlap), silk, tweeds and woolstrand can be stuck to a paper backing for use as wallcoverings. Similar products include exotica like grasscloth and suede wallcoverings. Hessian is available in a range of dyed colours, or *au naturel* which is intended to be overpainted. They need great care in hanging, and should be vacuum-cleaned regularly to remove surface dust. For spot-cleaning, it is best to use a dry-cleaning solvent rather than water.

ESTIMATING WALLCOVERINGS (WALLS)																	
Distance around room																	
9m	10m	12m	13m	14m	15m	16m	17m	19m	20m	21m	22m	23m	25m	26m	27m	28m	30m
30ft	34ft	38ft	42ft	46ft	50ft	54ft	58ft	62ft	66ft	70ft	74ft	78ft	82ft	86ft	90ft	94ft	98ft

Height

2.15–2.30m

7–7½ft: 4(7), 5(7), 5(8), 6(9), 6(10), 7(11), 7(12), 8(12), 8(13), 9(14), 9(15), 10(16), 10(17), 11(17), 12(18), 12(19), 13(20), 13(21)

2.30–2.45m

7½–8ft: 5(7), 5(8), 6(9), 6(9), 7(11), 7(12), 8(12), 8(13), 9(14), 9(15), 10(16), 10(17), 11(18), 11(19), 12(20), 13(20)-13(21), 14(22)

2.45–2.60m

8–8½ft: 5(7), 5(8), 6(9), 7(10), 7(11), 8(12), 9(13), 9(14), 10(15), 10(16), 11(17), 12(18), 12(19), 13(20), 14(21), 14(22), 15(23), 15(24)

2.60–2.75m

8½–9ft: 5(8), 5(9), 6(10), 7(11), 7(12), 8(13), 9(14), 9(15), 10(16), 10(17), 11(18), 12(19), 12(20), 13(21), 14(22), 14(23), 15(24), 15(25)

2.75–2.90m

9–9½ft: 6(8), 6(9), 7(10), 7(11), 8(13), 9(14), 9(15), 10(16), 10(17), 11(18), 12(19), 12(20), 13(21), 14(22), 14(23), 15(24), 15(25), 16(26)

2.90–3.05m

9½–10ft: 6(9), 6(10), 7(11), 8(12), 8(13), 9(14), 10(15), 10(17), 11(18), 12(19), 12(20), 13(21), 14(22), 14(23), 15(24), 16(25), 16(27), 17(28)

3.05–3.20m

10–10½ft: 6(9), 7(10), 8(11), 8(13), 9(14), 10(15), 10(16), 11(17), 12(18), 13(20), 13(21), 14(22), 15(23), 16(24), 16(25), 17(27), 18(28), 19(29)

The measurement around the room includes all windows and doorway. Note that UK rolls are given first with the number of US rolls following in brackets.

PASTES FOR PAPERHANGING

Buying the right paste for the wallcovering you have chosen is quite simple – it tells you what to use on the roll. Generally speaking, you can use any cold-water powder paste to hang 'whites' – lining paper, woodchip and relief wallcoverings – plus ordinary wallpapers and flocks. Vary the strength according to the weight of the paper – heavyweights and embossed types need a thicker paste than thin lightweights.

For any wallcovering that is impervious to moisture, such as washables and vinyls, you need a paste containing a fungicide. This stops mould growing in the paste as it dries out after the wallcovering has been hung.

Many washables and vinyls are also available ready-pasted; you simply immerse the cut length in a special soaking tray positioned against the skirting board (baseboard), then draw it up onto the wall and hang it in the usual way. It is a good idea to have a small quantity of ordinary paste mixed up ready for use when hanging ready-pasted papers; edges and seams can dry out before you have completed trimming and hanging awkward lengths, and may need a little extra paste to make them stick.

For most paper-backed fabrics the manufacturers recommend using a special heavy-duty, ready-mixed tub paste.

If papering bare plaster walls you will need to apply size to the surface first. Buy purpose-made size or use diluted wallpaper paste; they will reduce the porosity of the plaster and will enable pasted paper to be slipped across the surface more easily.

Lastly, you will need a special overlap adhesive, sold ready-mixed in tubes, to stick overlaps with vinyls and washables as their plastic surfaces reject ordinary paste.

GETTING READY TO START WORK

Do your estimating carefully so you can buy enough wallcovering for the job from the same batch; the charts here will help you to calculate the quantities you need. Check that the numbers on the individual roll labels are all the same; rolls from different batches may not match perfectly for colour.

Read the instructions on the roll, with particular reference to the type of paste to be used, whether the wall should be sized before paperhanging begins, and the time the paper should be left to soak after pasting. Remember to allow the same amount of soaking time for each length, so they stretch by the same amount. Ignore this, and you will have trouble matching patterns.

Check the type of pattern match. If it has a large pattern repeat or is a drop pattern, you may waste more paper than usual in cutting the lengths, and it may be wise to buy one or two extra rolls to be on the safe side. It is always worth having some paper left over at the end of the job anyway, so you can patch any damage that might occur in the future.

If you have to remove fixtures such as shelves, curtain tracks and wall lights, poke a match or a nail into the wallplugs to mark the screw positions for easy relocation when you have finished decorating. Finally, clear the room of furniture as far as possible, and get your paperhanging tool kit ready.

CEILINGS		
Distance round room		**No of**
m	**ft**	**rolls**
10	33	2(2)
11	36	2(3)
12	39	2(3)
13	42	3(3)
14	46	3(4)
15	49	4(5)
16	52	4(5)
17	55	4(6)
18	58	5(6)
19	62	5(7)
20	65	5(8)
21	68	6(8)
22	72	7(9)
23	75	7(10)

Note that the number of UK rolls are given first with the US equivalent following in brackets.

EQUIPMENT

You need a number of general-purpose and specialist tools to hang wallcoverings. The first, and one of the most important, is a plumb line: basically a length of thin cord with a pointed weight attached to one end, it is suspended from the top of each wall to give a true vertical guideline against which the first length of wallcovering is hung.

You can buy one or improvise by tying some string to a heavy object such as a bolt. If buying one, it is a good idea to choose what is called a chalk line. This coats the cord with fine coloured chalk powder as it is drawn out

of its holder. Pin the free end to the top of the wall (or ask someone to hold it there for you), then hold the cord taut against the wall surface, pull it away from the wall and let it snap back to leave a marked line. You can use it to mark your starting lines when papering ceilings too.

Next, you will need a steel tape measure for measuring the length to which each strip of wallcovering will be cut, plus a pencil for marking the cutting lines. Add a trimming knife or a pair of scissors for cutting the paper to length; long-bladed paperhanging shears are worth investing in if you do a lot of paperhanging.

Unless you are hanging a ready-pasted wallcovering or using a ready-mixed paste, you will need a clean bucket plus an improvised stirrer to mix the paste. To paste each length use any large paint brush or buy a special long-bristled pasting brush.

Last but not least, it is well worth investing in a purpose-made pasting table on which to lay the lengths as you paste them. These tables are made from hardboard or plywood on a light wooden or metal frame, and fold away neatly for easy storage.

If you are hanging a ready-pasted wallcovering, you can dispense with the paste bucket, pasting brush and table

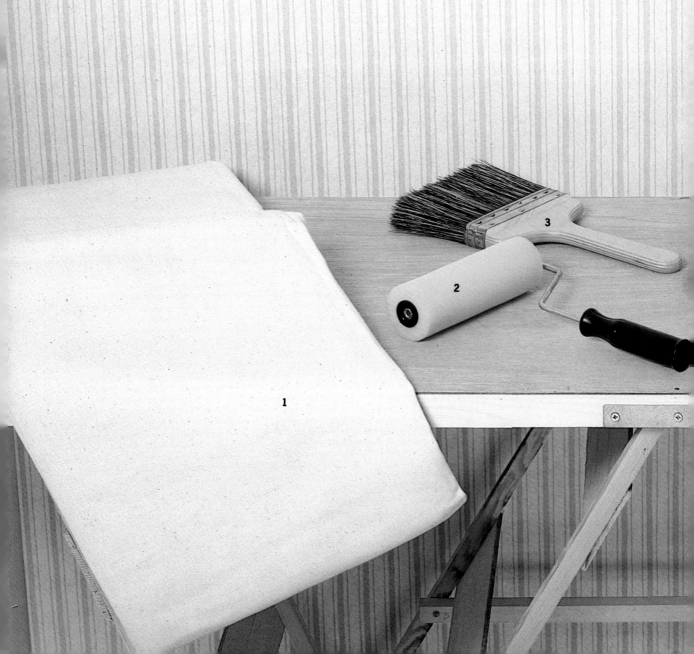

(although a pasting table is always useful for laying out and marking the lengths). All you need is an expanded polystyrene soaking trough in which to immerse the rolled-up lengths of wallcovering.

If you are hanging a wallcovering that requires the wall to be pasted, you will get smooth, even coverage by applying the paste with a foam-sleeved paint roller rather than a brush. Load it by pouring paste into the roller tray, just the same as when painting.

For hanging most types of wallcovering you need a special paperhanging brush. This has a wide set of soft bristles which are used to stroke and dab the wallcovering into place. If you are hanging washable or vinyl wallcoverings, you can use a sponge instead, but nothing works quite as effectively as the proper tool for the job. Use your paperhanging shears to trim the hung lengths at top and bottom and round any obstacles.

With your new wallcovering on the wall, the final tool you may need is a seam roller. This has a boxwood or plastic wheel which you run along the seams to ensure a good bond; however, it cannot be used on embossed or heavily textured wallcoverings because the roller will flatten the relief.

WALLPAPERING EQUIPMENT

For hanging most wallcoverings you will need paperhanging shears, a pasting brush or roller, a plumb line, a paperhanging brush and a seam roller. Add a trimming knife plus a pencil and tape measure for cutting the wallcovering to length.

1 **Dust sheet**
2 **Roller for pasting walls**
3 **Paste brush**
4 **Paperhanging brush**
5 **Seam rollers**
6 **Cutting knife**
7 **Paperhanging shears**
8 **Plumb line**
9 **Wallcoverings**
10 **Pasting table**

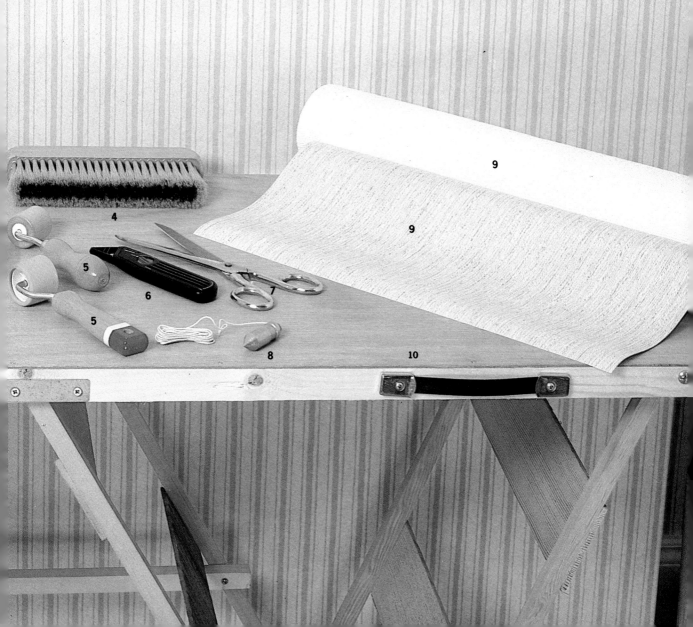

PAPERING WALLS

Paperhanging is one of the most satisfying of decorating jobs, for the simple reason that you get results so quickly. Once the preparation is over, whole walls can be covered in next to no time. The only awkward part is coping with obstacles – window reveals, light switches, sockets (receptacles), radiators and so on – and this section explains how to cope with these as well as covering the basic paperhanging techniques.

BASIC PROCEDURE

If you have never hung wallpaper before, it is a good idea to start your paperhanging career with a vinyl wallcovering. Vinyl is a better choice than ordinary wallpaper because it is far more tolerant of rough, inexperienced handling – it will not tear, and does not stretch much either so pattern matching is easier to achieve.

Set up the pasting table, mix up the paste and you are ready to start. Measure the wall height, add on about 100mm (4in) to allow for trimming and cut the paper to length. Mark the back to indicate which end of the length is the top.

Now position the length so the top is just overlapping the left-hand end of the pasting table (assuming you are right-handed; reverse this if you are left-handed), and draw it towards you so that one edge is in line with the near table edge.

Start brushing on the paste, spreading it out towards the top and the near side edge. When you have pasted as much as you can, push the paper away from you so the opposite edge is lined up with the far side of the table, and paste that edge too. This technique ensures good paste coverage without getting any paste on the table and as a result onto the face of the paper. This may not matter with a vinyl, but it could spell disaster for ordinary wallpaper and for more exotic coverings such as silk or grasscloth.

Next, draw up the middle of the pasted area to form a concertina fold, pasted side to pasted side, leaving the top 300mm (12in) or so uncovered – this will be the first part you stick to the wall. Carry on pasting and folding in this way until the length is completely pasted, and leave it to become supple for a few minutes. Soaking time varies from paper to paper; always check the wrapper for precise details.

PASTING AND FOLDING

1 Align the wallcovering on your pasting table so you can brush paste out to the edges of the length without getting any on the table.

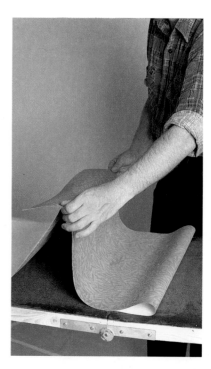

2 Fold the length up concertina-fashion on the pasting table with the top of the length uppermost.

PLUMBING A LINE

The one vital rule when paperhanging – ignore it at your peril – is to hang each length to a true vertical. If you do not do this, you will get very odd results at corners, patterns will not match and, worst of all, any motifs in the design that are repeated horizontally will actually seem to be climbing up the wall when viewed against ceiling lines or skirting (baseboards).

So mark a plumbed vertical line on the wall where you intend to start hanging, about 25mm (1in) less than the width of the paper away from the room corner. This

allows a narrow tongue of paper to turn onto the next wall and ensures that a joint cannot open up in the corner (see below).

You should mark a fresh plumb line every time you turn a corner. The reason for this is that few corners are perfectly plumb, and if you do not check the vertical your work will soon begin to run out of true.

Of course, if the room corner *is* true, you will be able to butt-join the next length in the usual way instead of overlapping it.

Slide one hand underneath the folded paper and carry it to the wall, with the pasted top edge away from you. Climb your steps or access platform and make sure the paper can drop freely down against the wall.

When in position, press the top edge of the length against the wall with your free hand, roughly aligning one edge with your plumbed line, and let a few of the pasted folds drop gently downwards. Slide the paper up so about 50mm (2in) laps onto the ceiling, and then align it accurately with the plumbed line. Brush the top part of the length firmly onto the wall with the paperhanging brush, working from the centre of the length out towards the edges to eliminate air bubbles. Then open up the remaining folds and smooth the rest of the length into place, down as far as the skirting board (baseboard).

Now trim the top and bottom of the length. Use long-bladed paperhanging shears for this – it is hard to get a neat cut with ordinary household scissors. First, draw the back of the blade along the angle to crease the paper; then peel the top away from the wall, cut along the line and brush the flap back into place. Repeat the process at the bottom of the length.

HANGING THE FIRST LENGTH

1 Carry the first length to the wall and press its top edge into position with the side edge aligned with the plumbed starting guideline. Press the top of the length into the wall–ceiling angle.

2 Unfold the rest of the length down the wall. Work downwards and from the centre of the length out towards the edges to brush the paper into place and smooth out any creases.

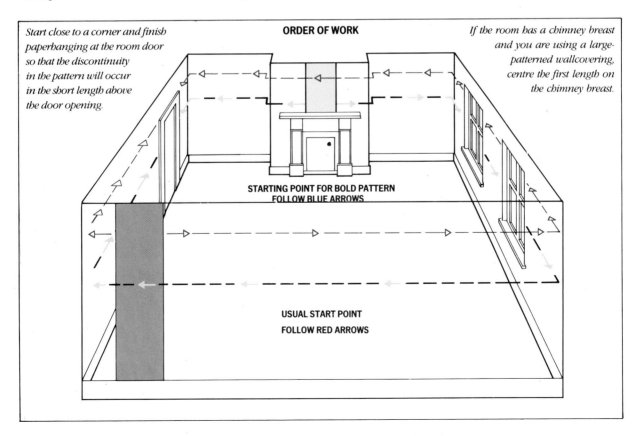

Start close to a corner and finish paperhanging at the room door so that the discontinuity in the pattern will occur in the short length above the door opening.

ORDER OF WORK

If the room has a chimney breast and you are using a large-patterned wallcovering, centre the first length on the chimney breast.

**STARTING POINT FOR BOLD PATTERN
FOLLOW BLUE ARROWS**

**USUAL START POINT
FOLLOW RED ARROWS**

TRIMMING

1 With the first length in place, use the paperhanging brush to push the wallcovering right into the wall–ceiling angle.

2 Then use a straightedge and a sharp trimming knife to cut through the wallcovering, and remove the waste. Alternatively, trim as below.

3 Use your paperhanging brush or shears to form a crease at the top or bottom of the length, which will act as a cutting guideline.

4 Peel the end of the length away and cut along the creased line with paperhanging shears. Then brush the end of the length back into place.

USING READY-PASTED WALLCOVERINGS

There are two main points to remember when using ready-pasted papers. Always soak the paper in the trough for precisely the time recommended by the manufacturer, and always use cold water. Many people think warm water will work better, but all it does is wash off the paste instead of just wetting it.

Cut the length to size, allowing extra for trimming as before. Roll the length up loosely with the pattern facing inwards, making sure the top edge is at the free end of the roll. Position the trough next to the wall and immerse the roll in the water for the recommended time. Then simply draw the length straight up from the trough onto the wall, allowing the water to drain back into the trough. Position, hang and trim as for ordinary wallpapers. Remember, however, that with ready-pasted wallcoverings you may need a little ordinary paste mixed up to stick down any corners or seams that have dried out during the hanging process.

1 Measure and cut the wallcovering to length and roll it up loosely (with the patterned face innermost) so the top of the length will be on the outside of the roll.

2 With the soaking trough next to the wall, immerse the roll for the recommended time. Then draw the top edge up and onto the wall surface.

76

PATTERN MATCHING

If hanging patterned paper, you need to check two points. The first is the pattern repeat – the distance down the length between repeating motifs. If this is large, there may be some wastage of paper when cutting each length to match the pattern with adjacent lengths. Next, check whether the pattern is a straight or a drop match. Straight patterns have the same design repeat at each side, but with drop patterns the design at one side of the length is half the repeat distance below the design at the other side. You must allow for this when cutting each length.

Having taken the pattern repeat and type into account, you can cut and paste length number two. Offer the top edge up to the wall as before, and slide it up to the ceiling and across to the edge of the first length. Match the pattern carefully, and brush the length into place. You may find that uneven stretch makes pattern matching difficult all the way down; if this occurs, as it may do with cheaper, thinner papers, aim for a good match at eye level to help disguise the problem. Finally, trim the top and bottom as before.

USING LARGE PATTERNS

1 If you are hanging a paper with a large pattern or a long pattern repeat, align adjacent edges at the top of the wall first.

2 If the paper stretches and you cannot get a perfect pattern match further down the wall, make the best match you can at eye level.

USING A SEAM ROLLER

With 'flat' wallcoverings, use a boxwood or plastic seam roller to ensure that edges adhere well to the wall.

TURNING CORNERS

Sooner or later, you will have to turn a corner, and it is important to do this correctly. Never try to turn more than about 50mm (2in) of paper onto the adjacent wall; it will almost certainly crease, and the turned edge will probably not be truly vertical anyway.

When you have hung the last complete length on the first wall, measure the distance to the corner. Unless it is within 50mm (2in) of the roll width, add about 25mm (1in) to the measurement and cut the strip to width. Do this with a trimming knife and ruler rather than with scissors to ensure a clean, straight cut. Save the other half of the strip, which you will then hang on the second wall.

Hang the strip as usual, matching the pattern carefully, and then brush the flap firmly into the corner. If it creases as you turn it, make small cuts at right angles to the edge of the flap to allow the paper to lie flat against the wall.

Having turned the corner successfully, you now need a second plumbed line, to ensure that lengths hung on the second wall will be truly vertical. Measure the width of the off-cut strip (left over from the corner turn) and subtract about 5mm (¼in). Measure this distance away from the turned flap and mark the plumb line. Hang the off-cut strip so it abuts the line and just overlaps the turned flap edge. With vinyls and washables, use a little overlap adhesive to stick the overlap down; ordinary paste will not work.

The same technique is used for turning external corners – at chimney breasts, for example. Hang the lengths on the face of the chimney breast first, turning a 25mm (1in) flap onto the side walls. Then paper the sides of the chimney breast, again turning a narrow flap onto the back wall of the alcove. Remember to plumb a new line every time you turn a corner.

With the corner safely negotiated, continue hanging full lengths in the usual way. Other difficulties you will encounter are things like doors, windows, radiators, shelves, mantelpieces, wall lights, light switches and socket outlets (receptacles); they can amount to a veritable obstacle course in some rooms.

TURNING EXTERNAL CORNERS

Never turn more than about 50mm (2in) of the wallcovering round an external corner, since the angle is unlikely to be truly vertical and the wallcovering will crease.

TURNING INTERNAL CORNERS

1 At internal corners, hang a narrow strip of the wallcovering on the first wall so it just turns the corner onto the adjacent wall surface.

2 Measure the width of the rest of the length, mark this on the second wall, plumb a line there and hang the piece to overlap the corner strip by about 6mm (¼in).

MOVABLE OBSTACLES

Rather like removing the handles when painting a door, it is necessary to unscrew and take down anything movable like shelving, curtain tracks and wall lights before paperhanging. To remove wall lights, turn off the power at the mains first and then unscrew and disconnect the fitting, taping any bare cable cores with PVC insulating tape before restoring the power. Whatever you take down, mark the wallplug position by inserting a matchstick in each screw hole. This will burst through the paper as you hang it, enabling easy location of the plug positions when putting everything back.

It is also best to remove radiators; this is actually less trouble than trying to paper round and behind them. Shut off the valves at each end, open the air vent, undo one valve coupling and drain the radiator contents into a shallow container. Then undo the other coupling, plug the outlets with cloths to prevent drips marking the floorcovering, and lift the radiator off its brackets. Remove these too, and mark the screw holes with matchsticks as before.

Light switches and socket outlets (receptacles) are semi-movable obstacles. To achieve a neat finish round them, loosen the faceplate fixing screws so you can ease the faceplates away from the wall surface and tuck trimmed tongues of paper behind them (see *Switches and Sockets*, page 80). *Always turn the power off at the mains first.* The one situation where you should not use this technique is when hanging metallic foil wallcovering, since these can conduct electricity. Instead of trimmed tongues, trim the wallcovering to finish flush with the edges of the faceplate.

WINDOW REVEALS

When you reach a window reveal, hang the first length that overlaps it as before and make horizontal cuts in line with the top and bottom of the reveal so you can turn the centre flap onto the reveal's side wall. Trim the vertical rear edge of the flap if it reaches the window frame; otherwise hang a narrow strip to fill the gap between the edge of the turned length and the frame. Next, cut a small patch to go on the underside of the top of the reveal, turn it up for about 25mm (1in) onto the face of the wall above the reveal and then brush the section that is already there down over it. Use overlap adhesive with washables and vinyls to get a good bond.

WORKING ROUND RADIATORS

1 If you are unable to remove the radiator, measure the height of the radiator brackets from the floor, and their distance from the edge of the last length hung, and make a cut-out.

2 Slide the length down behind the radiator so the cut-out fits round the bracket, and use a slimline paint roller to press it into place.

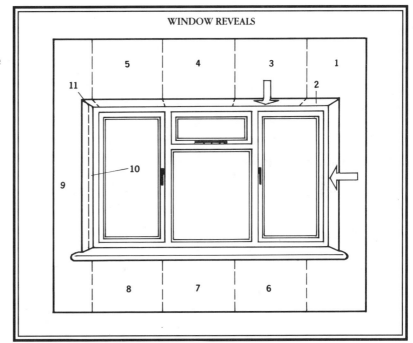

WINDOW REVEALS

A useful trick when hanging an ordinary printed paper, or one which will be painted over, is to carefully tear the edges of the overlapping pieces to form a feathered edge which will lie completely flat, forming an almost invisible join. With patterned or embossed papers, you obviously have to position the patch so the patterns match, and with patterned varieties the exposed feathered edge must be torn carefully to avoid exposing the backing paper.

Next, hang short lengths above and below the window, maintaining the pattern match

PAPERING AROUND A WINDOW REVEAL

This may appear quite tricky: follow the numbered sequence shown on the diagram above for perfect results.

throughout, until you can hang another complete length at the other side of the window reveal. Trim this as before (with a strip at the side of the reveal, if necessary), and fill in with another patch on the reveal underside. Use the same technique for recessed door openings.

SWITCHES AND SOCKETS (RECEPTACLES)

When you come across a light switch or socket outlet (receptacle), turn off the power and loosen the faceplate as mentioned earlier. Then let the paper hang over it, pierce it over the middle of the faceplate and make four cuts out towards the corners. Cut off the tongues so formed, leaving about 6mm (¼in) of paper which you can then tuck neatly behind the faceplate. Finally, tighten the fixing screws and restore the power. Do not use this technique if hanging metallic foil.

DOOR OPENINGS

Where there is an architrave moulding round a door opening, simply hang the paper so it overlaps the door opening, make a diagonal release cut up towards the top corner of the architrave at each side of the door and mark and trim the paper to fit round it.

WORKING ROUND SOCKETS

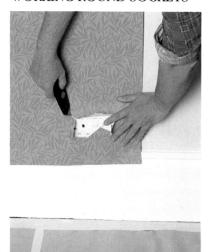

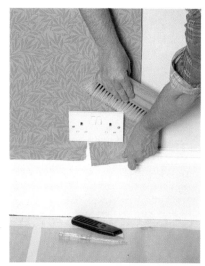

1 Paper over switches and socket outlets (receptacles), mark their outlines through the paper and make diagonal cuts out to the corners.

2 With the power off, loosen the faceplate screws and tuck the trimmed tongues of the wallcovering behind the faceplates. Tighten the screws.

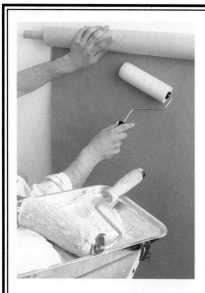

HANGING WALL FABRICS

It is often easier to hang wide paper-backed fabrics by pasting the wall (using a paint roller to ensure even coverage) and then rolling the material into place (above).

Overlap joins, then cut through each overlap with a sharp knife against a steel straight-edge for a really neat seam (right).

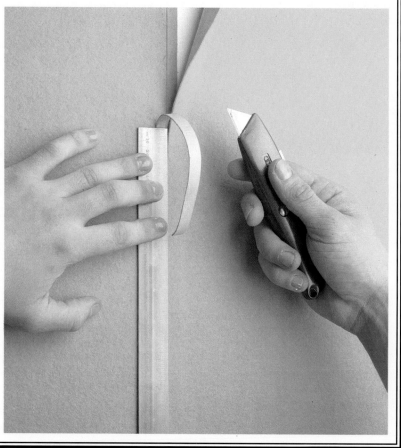

COPING WITH ARCHWAYS

1 Paper the face wall surrounding the arch first, trimming the wallcovering to follow the curved edge with a sharp cutting knife.

2 Then cut a strip of paper to cover the underside of the arch and brush it into place so its rear edge just overlaps the back of the recess.

3 Make a template of the rear wall with newspaper, and use this to cut a piece of wallcovering to fit. Brush this carefully into place.

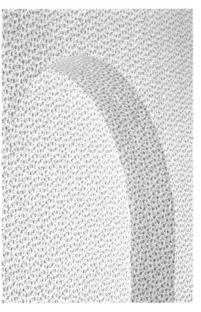

4 The completed recess. Always choose a wallcovering with a very small pattern and no discernible pattern match when decorating arches.

BUILT-IN OBSTACLES

The other problem you are likely to come up against is the built-in type – fitted furniture, for example, or a fire surround. Here, you should mark and trim the paper so it fits neatly into the angle between feature and wall. With irregular shapes like an ornate mantelshelf, make cuts into the edge of the paper so you can mark and trim each tongue in turn without creasing the paper unduly. This is a typical situation where some extra paste, held in a mug and applied with a small paint brush, will help to stick down any edges or tongues that are likely to have dried out while trimming to fit.

FINISHING TOUCHES

Practice makes perfect, but until you have become an experienced paperhanger there are a couple of tips that will help you get better results. One, which you can use on all but embossed papers, is to use a seam roller to ensure that seams lie flat. If they persist in lifting, ease them away from the wall and brush a little more paste behind them before pressing them back into place.

The second tip concerns blisters. You may find a number of these when the paper is first hung, but as long as they are small this is nothing to worry about; they will flatten out eventually as the paste dries. But there may be one or two larger blisters which usually indicate that you have missed pasting that area. The solution is to make two cuts in the paper at right angles using a razor blade or sharp craft knife, so you can fold back the tongues and brush on some paste before bedding them back onto the wall. The cuts will be almost invisible, especially if they are made to follow elements of the pattern.

PAPERING CEILINGS

Many people are terrified at the prospect of papering a ceiling. At first sight the job may seem particularly tricky, involving wrestling with unmanageable lengths of sticky paper while trying to make it hang upside down on the ceiling surface. In fact, apart from the surface being horizontal instead of vertical, it is really just a large flat wall, with far fewer obstructions to cope with than found on the walls of a typical room. All you have to master is the art of handling the paper while you coax it into position.

CHOOSING THE WALLPAPER

You can use any type of wallpaper – plain, washable, vinyl, relief – to paper a ceiling. However, for your first attempt it is a good idea to choose a fairly heavy (and therefore strong) paper with a random pattern, so you don't have to worry about tearing it or matching a pattern as you work. Perhaps the best choice would be either a relief type which can be painted afterwards, or else a vinyl wallcovering, which has the additional advantage of providing a ceiling surface that is easily washable.

If you do opt for a pattern, think carefully about which way to hang it. The traditional rules for papering ceilings say that you should hang the lengths parallel with the window wall. In the old days seams between lengths were overlapped slightly instead of being butt-jointed, and so working in this way prevented the overlaps from casting noticeable shadows on the ceiling surface. Nowadays, there is no reason not to work at right angles to the window wall, especially in a long thin room, since you will then be handling shorter and more manageable lengths of wallpaper. Consider too how many complete lengths you will get out of a roll; working in one direction rather than the other may mean a lot more wastage.

PAPERING A CEILING

1 Paste the first length as for walls, and fold it in a continuous concertina to make it easier to unfurl across the ceiling surface.

2 Working to a pencil guideline on the ceiling, drawn just less than the roll width away from the side wall, offer up the end of the length. (Note the safe use of access equipment.)

3 Press the end of the first length into the wall–ceiling angle with the paperhanging brush, leaving a small amount for trimming.

4 Start to unfurl the length across the ceiling, brushing it into place as you go. Note the turn onto the side walls, which will be trimmed later.

5 Use a pencil or the blades of the paperhanging shears to mark the trimming line on the wallcovering along the side wall.

6 Peel back the wallcovering carefully along the long edge and trim off the waste carefully along the marked line. Then brush the edge back into place.

7 Follow the same marking and cutting procedure to trim the two ends of the first length, and brush them back into the wall–ceiling angle.

8 Brush the second length into place alongside the first one, matching the pattern if there is one, and trim the ends as before.

9 Use a damp sponge to remove any traces of paste from the adjacent wall surfaces and also from the wallcovering itself.

TOOLS AND EQUIPMENT

As far as tools are concerned, the same kit is needed as for basic paperhanging. The only other tool required is a screwdriver, to take down the ceiling lights – a far easier prospect than trying to fit the wallpaper round them. Turn off the power at the main fusebox, then either remove the lighting circuit fuse or switch off the miniature circuit breaker (MCB) before unscrewing and disconnecting the light fitting. If you have a pendant light, simply unscrew the rose cover and disconnect the pendant flex from it. Restore the power to the other circuits in the house; if you need light in the room you are working in, it can then be provided by means of table or standard lights plugged into socket outlets (receptacles).

ACCESS EQUIPMENT

The most awkward part of papering a ceiling is reaching it. Since you need to be able to move from one end of each length to the other as you hang it, it is no good trying to perch on chairs or small steps. What you really need is a continuous low-level work platform which can be positioned directly

beneath each length, allowing you to walk its length unobstructed. Professional decorators use trestles and staging or the components of a slot-together platform tower for this; the amateur can hire these, or, alternatively, set up one or two scaffold boards running between the treads of household steps or small homemade hop-ups.

To avoid accidents, make sure the boards are secured to the supports. Either use woodworking clamps, or drill holes in both boards and supports and drop in a bolt to lock the two together. You do not need a nut. This arrangement makes it easy to dismantle and reposition the working platform as you tackle successive lengths.

STARTING WORK

If your ceiling is newly plastered, brush on a coat of size before you start paperhanging. This seals the porous plaster surface, preventing the paste from drying out too quickly and also allowing the paper to be 'slipped' into position for seam and pattern matching. You can usually use ordinary wallpaper paste for this; simply dilute it with more water than if you were making it up as

paste. If the paste is suitable for use as size, the correct dilution will be given on the packet. Choose size which incorporates a fungicidal paste if you are hanging washable or vinyl wallcoverings.

The next step is to decide which way to hang the paper. Having done this, pin a chalked string line across the ceiling parallel with the direction you have chosen. Position it about 25mm (1in) less than the width of the wallpaper away from the wall, to allow the long edge to be trimmed when the length has been hung if the walls will be painted, or to be turned onto the wall surfaces if these will also be papered. Once in position, snap the string against the ceiling surface to leave a clear guideline visible.

Next, measure the width of the room and cut your first length, allowing an extra 50mm (2in) at each end for trimming. If the paper used does not have a pattern match, you can save some time and use the first length as a guide to cut all the others to length at this stage too.

USING ACCESS EQUIPMENT

Use either trestles and staging (or boards) or a length of boarding and two step ladders for your working platform. Whenever possible, enlist the help of a second person to support the free end of the ceiling paper while you position and brush the other end in place against your guideline.

PASTING AND FOLDING

Since you will be handling longer pieces of paper than you would when papering a wall, it is important to paste and fold the lengths correctly. Start at one end, and paste an area almost as long as your pasting table. Then fold this up into a series of pleats, pasted side to pasted side, so that each fold is about 450mm (18in) wide; leave a short fold pasted side uppermost on top of the pile. Move the paper along so that the concertina section is at one end of the table. Paste further sections, and form pleats as before. When you reach the far end of the length, take the last fold to meet the short one on top of the pile. The paper edges should meet without paste getting onto the front of the paper.

HANGING THE FIRST LENGTH

Pick up the folded length carefully and slip a spare roll of paper under it for support as you carry it to your work position. Peel away the last fold you made and let it hang free, then offer up the pasted end of the first fold to the ceiling and brush it into place so it overlaps onto the wall at right angles to the direction of hanging. Slip it across so its outer long edge lines up with the chalk line, and brush the first metre/yard of paper into place.

Now move back along the working platform, letting more paper unfold from the pile, and brush a further section into position. Check that it is still aligned with the chalk line, and that its other long edge is brushed well into the wall–ceiling angle.

Complete hanging the first length by brushing the other end into the angle between the ceiling and the opposite wall.

Subsequent lengths are hung in exactly the same way, with one long edge carefully butted up against the edge of the previous length (and with the pattern, if there is one, carefully matched). The last length you hang will probably not be a full-width strip; cut it down in width before pasting it, allowing about 25mm (1in) extra width so its long edge can be neatly trimmed against the side wall or turned onto it as appropriate.

When each length has been hung, trim the ends by creasing the paper into the wall–ceiling angle, peeling it carefully away and cutting neatly along the crease line. Repeat the creasing and cutting process down the long edge of the first and last lengths hung.

Do not worry about any blisters that appear at this stage; they will probably flatten out as the paper dries.

DEALING WITH CEILING FIXTURES

Where a length covers a light position, a little careful cutting is required. Brush the paper into place so it covers the rose or cable position, then pierce the paper in line with the centre of the rose. Peel it away carefully, and make radial cuts from the hole outwards to just beyond the outline of the rose itself. Brush the length back into place, allowing the triangular tongues of paper to hang downwards round the rose. Then trim each one off flush with the edge of the rose baseplate and brush it back against the ceiling surface. The cut edges will be completely concealed when the rose cover (or light fitting) is replaced. Use a variation on

LIGHT FITTINGS

If you cannot remove ceiling roses before papering, pierce the paper in line with the centre of the rose, make radial cuts outwards and then trim off the tongues of paper.

this technique to cope with larger obstacles such as decorative ceiling centres.

With all the lengths hung and trimmed, check that all the seams are well stuck down by running a seam roller along them. Do not use a seam roller with a relief or embossed pattern wallcovering, as it will flatten the three-dimensional surface effect. Instead, use the paperhanging brush with a firm stippling action to ensure that all the seams are well secured to the ceiling.

PAPERING STAIRWELLS

The biggest difficulty with papering stairwells lies in rigging up suitable access equipment without completely blocking the stairs. The best solution is usually a combination of short ladders, steps and scaffold boards; nail battens (furring strips) to stair treads to prevent ladders and steps from slipping, and rope boards to treads and to each other. As an alternative, hire a narrow slot-together access tower and use its components to build a suitable platform.

Start paperhanging with the longest 'drop'. Measure its length carefully, remembering to allow for the slope of the skirting board (baseboard) at its lower end. Then paste and fold the length as for ceiling paper, and carry it to the top of the wall.

Long lengths will stretch if allowed to hang unsupported, so have a helper available to take the weight of the lower half of the drop while you position the top half. Then descend from the platform and complete hanging the lower part of the length. If pattern matching proves difficult because of paper stretch, go for the best match you can at about eye level, viewed from the flight itself.

USING FRIEZES AND BORDERS

These are narrow strips of printed paper or vinyl with designs and colours that complement those in wallcoverings and fabrics from the same manufacturer. A frieze can be hung on the wall at ceiling level, at picture-rail height or above or below a dado (chair) rail, while borders are generally used to frame some feature of the room – a door or window opening, for example – or to form framed panels on the walls or ceiling as a decorative feature.

Friezes and borders are increasingly being sold in self-adhesive form, although those that need pasting are still available. The latter are fine on painted surfaces or surfaces decorated with an ordinary patterned wallpaper, but will not stick satisfactorily to washable or vinyl wallcoverings.

To put up a frieze or border, draw light pencil guidelines on the wall or ceiling surface with the aid of a spirit level (and a plumb line for border panels on walls). Then paste the strip, taking care to keep the face clean, fold it up concertina-fashion, carry it to the wall and brush it into place. If you have to abut successive lengths, overlap the two, align the pattern and cut through both pieces with a sharp trimming knife and a

USING ACCESS EQUIPMENT IN STAIRWELLS

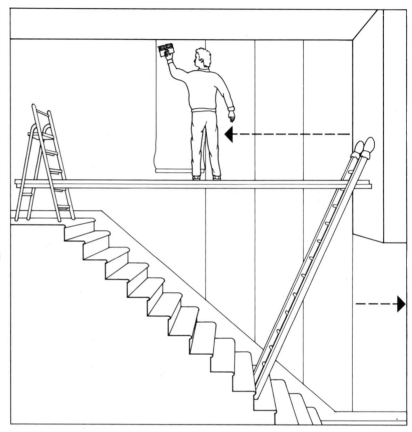

STRAIGHT STAIRWELLS
Position a ladder against the head wall and steps on the landing and run a board between the two for your working platform.

Always hang the longest drop first, measuring its length carefully to allow for the slope in the skirting board (baseboard). Now work up the flight towards the landing.

straightedge. Discard the offcuts and brush the ends back into place for an invisible join. For border panels, overlap the strips at right angles, then cut through both strips to leave perfect mitred corners.

If you are using a self-adhesive type, simply peel off some of the backing paper and position the end of the strip. Then work along the length, peeling and sticking as you go, always working to the guidelines.

MAKING A BORDER PANEL
Mark the panel outline on the wall and brush the first length into place. Then place the next length at right angles to the first, overlapping it so the pattern matches. Use a cutting knife and metal straightedge to cut through the corner overlap at 45°, peel off the waste and use a seam roller to bond the strips back to the wall.

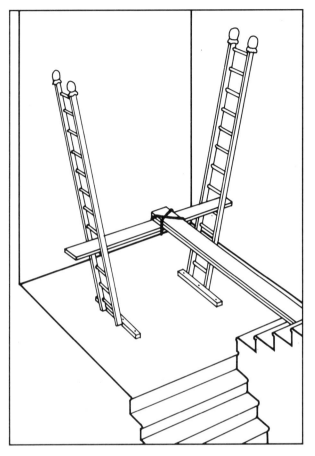

HALF-LANDINGS
*Use two ladder sections plus scaffold boards
to form a working platform. Battens (furring
strips) on the floor prevent the ladders from
slipping.*

QUARTER-LANDINGS
*Use a ladder section plus steps and hop-ups
to build a platform at the required level. Put
pads on the ladder stiles to protect the walls.*

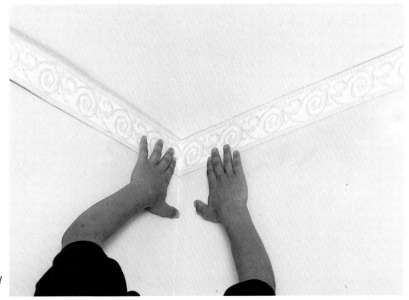

PUTTING UP BORDERS
*Hang a border to a marked horizontal
guideline unless it is following the ceiling
line or a picture rail. Use self-adhesive types
over vinyls and washable wallcoverings, and
pasted ones on painted walls.*

USING LINING PAPER

Where wall or ceiling surfaces are uneven, porous or covered in hairline cracks, they should be covered with lining paper first. Lining paper is a plain, absorbent material that disguises defects and provides the perfect base for all types of wallcovering. To avoid the risk of joins between lengths coinciding with those in the wallcovering, lining paper is hung in horizontal strips.

The technique is quite simple. You cut the first length to match the width of the wall being lined, with an allowance for end trimming, paste it and hang it at the top of the wall, turning about 25mm (1in) of paper onto the ceiling if this will be papered too.

Fold the length concertina-fashion on the pasting table, then start hanging it at the right-hand side of the wall if you are right-handed, or at the left side if you are left-handed. Position the end of the length against the wall, then allow the rest of the concertina to unfold slowly as you brush the paper into position. Trim the ends neatly into the angles at the room corners.

Hang subsequent lengths in the same way, leaving a very slight gap between the adjacent long edges. The last length at skirting-board (baseboard) level will probably be a narrowish strip; cut it a little over-size, then hang it and trim its lower edge to just clear the top of the board.

USING RELIEF WALLCOVERINGS

1 Paste all relief wallcoverings generously so the paste fills the embossing. Concertina long lengths or fold short lengths, as here, back to back and leave to soak for the recommended time before hanging.

◀ **2** Brush the wallcovering into place carefully so as not to flatten the embossing. Trim as usual, but do not use a seam roller.

▶ **3** When the paste has dried out fully, decorate the surface of the wall-covering with emulsion (latex) or solvent-based (alkyd) paint.

REPAIRING WALLCOVERINGS

The most common damage that wallcoverings will sustain is a tear resulting from carelessly moved furniture or some other impact. Another cause of tears is lifting seams which have been left unattended and been accidentally caught and ripped. Until you next intend to redecorate, all you can do is try to conceal the damage.

If the wallcovering has a jagged tear, attempt to stick it back down with a little wallpaper paste or some household adhesive; use sticky tape to secure it on washables and vinyls until the adhesive sets.

If the torn piece has disappeared and you have some of the wallcovering left over, try patching the damage. Place an offcut of the original wallpaper over the hole and match the pattern (if there is one) carefully. Cut through both layers of paper to form a patch. Remove the offcut and carefully lift away the torn wallcovering from the wall. Then paste the new patch up in its place.

If you find seams beginning to lift as time goes by, stick them down again before they become torn. Again, use ordinary paste or overlap adhesive as appropriate, and roll the seams flat with a seam roller to ensure a good bond is achieved.

PATCHING

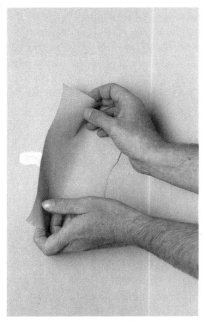

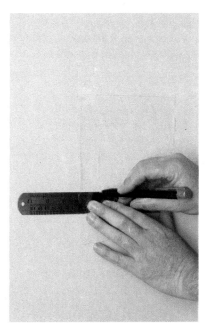

1 To disguise a torn patch, place an offcut of the original wallcovering over the damaged area, aligning the pattern (if there is one) carefully.

2 Cut through both layers of paper with a sharp cutting knife and a straightedge to form a patch that will match the pattern.

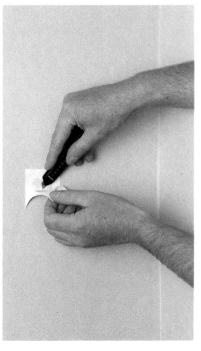

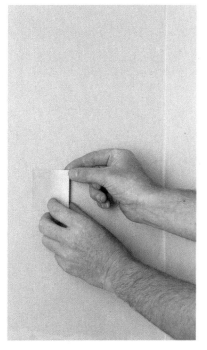

LIFTING SEAMS

If seams and edges lift, brush a little extra paste under them and press them back. Use special overlap adhesive with washables and vinyls.

3 Remove the offcut, then use a sharp knife to lift the original torn wallcovering from the wall. Scrape off any backing paper that is left behind.

4 Paste the patch with a little wallpaper paste and press it into position. Use a seam roller to flatten the joins all round the edges.

ORDER OF WORK

This sequence of events outlines the main stages involved in a full room redecoration programme. Use it as a guide to producing a detailed checklist for each room you are tackling.

1 SURVEY THE ROOM
- Check ceilings for stains, cracks, signs of bowing, old distemper
- Check walls for damp, cracks, loose plaster, damaged mouldings
- Check doors and windows for smooth operation, rot, rust or mould
- Make list of essential repairs

2 COLLECT TOOLS AND MATERIALS
- Choose new decorations
- Make list of tools and equipment
- Buy new decorations, and buy or hire any tools and equipment required

3 CLEAR THE ROOM
- Remove all movable furniture
- Take down wall-mounted fixtures and fittings, ceiling lights etc. *Always turn off the electricity before removing or loosening light fittings, switches and sockets (receptacles).*
- Put dust sheets over immovable fixtures and fittings
- Cover remaining floorcoverings

4 CLEAN MAIN SURFACES
- Strip old draughtproofing materials from doors and windows
- Remove black mould from windows
- Vacuum-clean room

5 STRIP UNWANTED DECORATIONS
- Remove old tiles/cladding (siding) etc
- Strip old wallcoverings
- Strip ceiling decorations
- Strip woodwork if necessary

6 MAJOR MODIFICATIONS
- Fit wiring for new lights, socket outlets (receptacles) etc
- Reposition existing light fittings
- Make plumbing alterations
- Fit/replace/remove fireplace
- Replace doors/windows
- Tackle damp/rot/insect damage
- Install new decorative mouldings

Note: If in doubt, always seek professional help for these tasks

7 CARRY OUT MINOR REPAIRS
- Patch wall/ceiling cracks
- Fill and sand damaged woodwork

8 CLEAN DOWN SURFACES
- Wash down and dry off all surfaces to be redecorated
- Vacuum-clean floor surface
- Reposition dust sheets

9 REDECORATE CEILING

10 REDECORATE WALLS
(Redecorate woodwork first – see 11 – if paperhanging)

11 REDECORATE WOODWORK AND TRIMS

12 REPLACE FITTINGS AND FIXTURES

SAFETY

Decorating is not a particularly dangerous activity as far as home improvement jobs go, but there are several hazards to watch out for.

ACCESS EQUIPMENT

Always make sure that any steps, ladders and access platforms you set up when decorating are level and secure. Tie or cramp horizontal boards to their supports so they cannot slip. Never lean out too far from steps or ladders in case you overbalance, and watch your footing when stepping up or down.

CHEMICALS

Take special care when using chemicals such as paint strippers, solvent thinners and brush cleaners, to ensure that you do not splash them on your skin or in your eyes. Read the instructions carefully and wear gloves and goggles when using them, especially if using them overhead.

DUST

Many preparation jobs involve the use of abrasive materials which can create a lot of dust. Wear a dust mask to avoid inhaling dust, and a pair of safety goggles to keep dust out of your eyes.

ELECTRICITY

When soaking and stripping old wallcoverings, either protect switches and socket outlets (receptacles) from water or turn off the power supply. ALWAYS turn off the power if removing faceplates or light fittings while decorating.

FUMES

Many paints, varnishes and stains dry by evaporation of a volatile solvent which can smell unpleasant in confined spaces and which some people find gives them headaches. Always ensure good natural ventilation when using these products. Remember that some are inflammable; do not smoke when using them.

RUBBISH

Always dispose of decorating debris safely. Bag up stripped wallcoverings, and deposit paint scrapings in a tin or glass container, not a plastic one. Dry solvent-soaked cloths before wrapping and disposing of them.

Left: *If using chemicals or a steam stripper, always ensure that your hands are protected with gloves and your eyes with safety goggles.*

Above: *If your work causes a dust problem, make sure you take the additional precaution of wearing a face mask.*

Left: *Always check and double-check that any access equipment in use has been correctly assembled and is perfectly safe. Hired trestles and boarding make a rock-steady working platform when papering ceilings.*

STOCKISTS AND SUPPLIERS

BASIC TOOLS AND EQUIPMENT

Black & Decker Ltd
Westpoint
The Grove
Slough
Berkshire SL1 1QQ
0753 511234

Hobbs & Co Ltd
88 Blackfriars Road
London SE1 8HA
071-928 1891

H S S Hire Group Ltd
25 Willow Lane
Mitcham
Surrey CR4 9AR
081-685 9900

Mosley-Stone
3 Morgan Way
Bowthorpe Industrial Estate
Bowthorpe
Norwich
Norfolk
NR5 9JJ
0603 743665

Plasplugs Ltd
Wetmore Road
Burton-on-Trent
Staffordshire DE14 1SD
0283 30303

W C Youngman
Stane Street
Slinford
Horsham
West Sussex RH13 7RD
0403 790456

PAINTS

Akzo Coatings plc
135 Milton Park
Abingdon
Oxfordshire OX14 4SB
0235 862226

Laura Ashley Ltd
150 Bath Road
Maidenhead
Berkshire SL6 4YS
0628 770345

Craig & Rose
Princes Road
Dartford
Kent DA2 6EE
0322 222481

Crown Berger Ltd
Crown House
Hollins Road
Darwen
Lancashire BB3 0BG
0254 704951

Dulux (ICI plc Paints Division)
Wexham Road
Slough
Berkshire SL2 5DS
0753 550000

International Paints
24–30 Canute Road
Southampton
Hants SO9 3AS
0703 226722

Kalon Decorative Products
Huddersfield Road
Birstall
Batley
West Yorkshire WF17 9XA
0924 477201

Macphersons Paints Ltd
Radcliff Road
Bury
Lancashire BL9 9NB
061 764 6030

Arthur Sanderson & Sons Ltd
100 Acres
Oxford Road
Uxbridge
Middx UB8 1HY
0895 238244

WALLCOVERINGS

Laura Ashley Ltd
150 Bath Road
Maidenhead
Berkshire SL6 4YS
0628 770345

Crown Berger Ltd
Crown House
Hollins Road
Darwen
Lancashire BB3 0BG
0254 704951

Designers Guild
3 Olaf Street
London W11 4BE
071-243 7300

Forbo-CP Ltd
Station Road
Cramlington
Northumberland NE23 8AQ
0670 718222

Forbo-CP Kingfisher Wallcoverings
Lune Mills
Lancaster
Lancashire LA1 5QN
0524 65222

Graham & Brown Ltd
PO Box 39
India Mill
Harwood Street
Blackburn
Lancashire BB1 3BR
0254 661122

Harlequin Wallcoverings
Cossington Road
Sileby
Nr Loughborough
Leicestershire LE12 7RU
0509 816575

Osborne and Little
49 Temperley Road
London SW12 8QE
081-675 2255

Arthur Sanderson & Sons Ltd
100 Acres
Oxford Road
Uxbridge
Middx UB8 1HY
0895 238244

Muriel Short Designs
Hewitts Estate
Elmbridge Road
Cranley
Surrey GU6 8LW
0483 271211

Storeys Decor
Southgate
White Lund
Morecambe
Lancashire
LA3 3DA
0524 65981

Tektura Ltd
4–10 Rodney Street
London
N1 9JH
071-837 8000

Today Interiors
Hollis Road
Grantham
Lincolnshire NG31 7QH
0476 74401

WOOD FINISHES

Akzo Coatings plc
135 Milton Park
Abingdon
Oxfordshire OX14 4SB
0235 862226

Cuprinol Ltd
Adderwell
Frome
Somerset BA11 1NL
0373 465151

Langlow Products Ltd
PO Box 32
Asheridge Road
Chesham
Buckinghamshire HP5 2QF
0494 784866

Roncraft
Thorncliff Park
Chapeltown
Sheffield
South Yorkshire S30 4YF
0742 467171

Rustins Ltd
Waterloo Road
London NW2 7TX
081-450 4666

Sadolin Nobel (UK) Ltd
Sadolin House
Meadow Lane
St Ives
Cambridgeshire PE17 4UY
0480 496868

AUSTRALIA

PAINTS

British Paints
9–29 Gow Street
Padstow
Sydney NSW
02 707 8222

Pascol Paints Australia Pty Ltd
PO Box 63
Rosebery
NSW 2018
02 669 2266

Taubmans
51 McIntyre Road
Sunshine
Victoria 3020
03 311 0211

WOOD FINISHES

Cabots, Kenbrock Australia Pty Ltd
1330 Ferntree Gully Road
Scoresby
Victoria 3179
03 765 2222

Sikkens (Tenaru Pty Ltd)
PO Box 768
Darlinghurst
Sydney
NSW 2010
02 357 4500

NORTH AMERICA

BASIC TOOLS AND EQUIPMENT

Black & Decker
Communications Department
702 East Joppa Road
Towson
Maryland 21286

Robert Bosch Power Tool Corporation
100 Bosch Blvd
New Bern
North Carolina 28562

Home Depot
2727 Paces Ferry Road
Atlanta
Georgia 30339
(404) 433–8211
**Also wallpaper supplies, specialty wallcoverings and paint

J C Penney
1301 Avenue of the Americas
New York
New York 10019
(800) 222–6161
**Also, wallpaper supplies, specialty wallcoverings, paints.

Porter Cable Corporation
4825 Highway 45 North
Jackson
Tennessee 38302

Sears Roebuck
Sears Tower
Chicago
Illinois 60684
(800) 366–3000

Skil Corporation
4300 West Peterson Avenue
Chicago
Illinois 60646

True Value Hardware
(800) 621–6025

WALLCOVERINGS

**Also available at above retailers

Border Home Wall Coverings
(800) 426–7336

North American Decorative Products Inc
1055 Clark Boulevard
Brompton
Ontario
Canada L6T 3W4

PAINT SUPPLIERS

**Also available at above retailers

Benjamin Moore
51 Chestnut Ridge Road
Montvale
New Jersey 07645
(201) 576-9600

Pratt & Lambert
75 Tonawanda Street
Buffalo
New York 14207
(716) 873–6000

Sherwin Williams
101 Prospect Avenue
N W Cleveland
Ohio 44115
(216) 566–2000

GLOSSARY

Abrasive paper Used to rub-down, smooth or key a surface prior to redecorating. Also known as sandpaper and glasspaper.

Alkyd paint *see* Solvent-based paint

Alkyd resin Ingredient used as a binder in modern solvent-based gloss and eggshell paints.

Aluminium wood primer Primer used on resinous hardwoods and to seal bituminous paints and stains.

Baseboard *see* Skirting

Batten (furring strip) Narrow strip of softwood.

Border Narrow strip of printed wallpaper, used to highlight features such as window openings or picture rails.

Bradawl A pointed tool for marking and making holes.

Caulking *see* Mastic

Cold chisel Large hardened chisel used to cut through masonry and plaster.

Cornice (crown molding) Decorative band of plaster or wood placed at wall–ceiling junction.

Cross-lining Hanging lining paper horizontally on wall surfaces prior to hanging another wallcovering over it.

Crown molding *see* Cornice

Distemper An old-fashioned wall paint no longer used, but often found beneath old wallpaper. It must be removed or sealed before being decorated over.

Dry wall *see* Plasterboard

Efflorescence White powdery deposit found on wall surfaces that are damp or which have not dried out after replastering work. It should be brushed off dry.

Eggshell paint Solvent-based (alkyd) paint which dries to a sheen rather than a high gloss.

Emulsion (latex) paint Water-based paint mainly used on wall and ceiling surfaces; thinned and washed from tools with water.

Filler Powder or ready-mixed product used to repair minor damage to wood, plaster and plasterboard (dry wall or gypsum board) surfaces.

French polish A high-gloss professional finish for furniture and wood.

Frieze Narrow strip of printed wallpaper, somewhat wider than a border, used to form decorative bands on walls.

Furring strip *see* Batten

Glasspaper *see* Abrasive paper

Glaze A transparent or semi-transparent colour applied over a base colour.

Gypsum board *see* Plasterboard

Knotting Shellac-based sealer used to cover knots in woodwork, preventing resin from oozing through and marring the finish.

Latex paint *see* Emulsion

Lath-and-plaster Wall or ceiling formed by nailing slim timber strips across joists or timber frames and filling with plaster.

Lining (liner) paper Plain wallpaper hung to provide a stable base for other wallcoverings.

Mastic (caulking) A sealer used to make waterproof and flexible joints.

Matt (flat) paint Paint that dries to a flat, non-reflective finish.

Mitre To cut two lengths of material (wood, plaster etc) at matching angles to form a corner joint.

Picture rail A narrow moulding fixed around a room below ceiling height.

Plasterboard (dry wall or gypsum board) Thin rigid board of plaster compressed between two layers of paper, used to form or cover walls, ceilings and partitions.

Plumb-bob Pointed weight, usually affixed to a line and suspended to determine a true vertical.

Primer Liquid used on many bare surfaces to seal them and provide a good base for undercoats and topcoats.

PVA (polyvinyl acetate) A chemical compound used in adhesives such as woodworking (white) glue. Diluted, it can be used as a sealer.

Ready-pasted wallcovering Wallcovering coated with dried paste, which is activated by immersing each length in a trough of water.

Relief wallcovering Embossed material designed to be overpainted once hung.

Sandpaper *see* Abrasive paper

Satin or silk finish paint Solvent- or water-based paint that dries to a slight sheen rather than a high-gloss finish.

Scrim Fine material or gauze used with filler or plaster to patch holes in plaster surfaces.

Size A dilute glue used to seal wall and ceiling surfaces before decorating with wallcoverings.

Skirting (baseboard) Edging of wood, plaster etc used to trim the base of a wall.

Solvent-based (alkyd) paint Paint mainly used on wood and metal; use white (mineral) spirit or turpentine substitute as a thinner and cleaning agent.

Textured finish Powder or ready-mixed compound applied to wall and ceiling surfaces and given a random or regular decorative texture.

Thixotropic (non-drip) paint Paint with a jelly-like consistency which does not drip or run on application.

Undercoat Paint applied between primer and topcoat in a three-coat paint system. Provides a good key for finishing coat.

Vinyl wallcovering Wallcovering with the design printed on a PVC layer which is stuck to a paper backing. The top layer can be stripped dry.

Washable wallpaper Printed paper with a clear plastic surface coating which can be washed and which must be broken up before the paper can be stripped.

Woodchip wallpaper Wallpaper containing coarse wood chips, designed to be overpainted once hung.

INDEX

PICTURE CREDITS

The authors and publishers would like to thank the following companies and their PR agencies for the loan of photographs used in this book.

Laura Ashley: page 35 t.
Marshall Cavendish: pages 12, 15 tl, 18, 26, 27 tl tc tr, 80 bl br, 85, 91 t.
Crown Berger: pages 2, 34, 29 t, 40 t b, 41, 42, 56, 61, 67.
Dulux: pages 6/7, 10, 20, 32, 33, 36 b, 37 b, 47, 107.
Forbo-Kingfisher: pages 39 b, 70.
Osborne and Little: pages 37 t, 38, 66.
Arthur Sanderson & Sons: page 36.

Key: t = top; b = bottom; l = left; r = right; c = centre.

ACKNOWLEDGEMENTS

The authors and publishers would like to thank the following companies and their PR agencies for their advice and the loan and/or provision of materials and equipment used in this book. See Stockists and Suppliers for addresses and telephone numbers.

Black & Decker Ltd
Craig & Rose
Crown Berger Ltd
Dulux
Hobbs & Co Ltd
H S S Hire Group Ltd
Mosley-Stone
North American Decorative Products Inc
Plasplugs
W C Youngman

Anness Publishing would also like to thank Roger and Samuel and the other private individuals who helped in the realisation of this book.